AND I
QUOTE

AND I
QUOTE

Derek Lambert

Arlington Books
Clifford Street Mayfair
London

AND I QUOTE
first published 1980 by
Arlington Books (Publishers) Ltd
3 Clifford Street Mayfair
London W.I.

© *Derek Lambert 1980*

Set in England by
Inforum Ltd Portsmouth
Printed and bound in England by
Biddles Ltd
Guildford and King's Lynn

British Library Cataloguing in Publication Data
Lambert, Derek
And I quote —
1. Lambert, Derek — Biography
Authors, English — 20th century — Biography
3. Journalists — Great Britain — Biography
I. Title
070' .92'4   PR6062.A47Z/

ISBN 0 85140 503 7

For Rupert Grayson
of whom it was once said

AUTHOR'S NOTE

In the interests of the narrative the chronology has been adjusted in a few sequences and the names of some of the participants have been changed.

I

I arrived in Fleet Street on a No. 11 bus displaying classic symptoms of an imminent nervous breakdown.

A heart-beat accelerating like a Formula One racing car coming out of a bend, the brand of anxiety experienced by a mass murderer awaiting the jury's verdict and a twitch that had explored the possibilities of most of my facial muscles before settling on my upper lip.

All with good reason. Behind me, as a reporter on various Provincial newspapers, lay three years of earnest endeavour devastated at regular intervals by journalistic calamities. (Who else can claim to have been fired on their twenty-first birthday for reporting a case of chicken-pox as an outbreak of small-pox?)

Ahead lay the awesome challenge of a job in the London office of the *Daily Mirror*, a tabloid as brash and brawling as it was technically sophisticated.

But these weren't the only considerations fueling my neurosis as I alighted from the bus and made my way up Fetter Lane, a tributary of Fleet Street, where the drab, pagoda-like offices of the *Mirror* were then located.

It was the autumn of 1953 and the decade was already set on a course of cataclysmic change. . . .

Queen Elizabeth II had been crowned that summer; the Tories were back in power after the post-war resurgence of the Labour Party; both the Americans and Russians had exploded Hydrogen bombs; General Dwight Eisenhower had become the first Republican President of the United States since 1932 and Joseph Stalin had died aged seventy-four.

Earlier in 1953 British mountaineers had conquered Everest, the Korean War had ended — and James Bond had arrived. Looking decidedly un-Bondish in my funereal overcoat (I had once been mistaken for an undertaker at a cremation), and a suit that steamed in damp weather, I felt singularly ill-equipped to chronicle the spell-binding happenings that surely lay ahead.

By the time I reached the courtyard outside the *Mirror* offices I had become convinced that I was the victim of a misunderstanding: rabbit shows, motoring courts and amateur dramatics were not, as I had been led to understand, the stuff of which international ace reporters were made.

I consulted my wrist-watch, 9.50 a.m. I had been instructed to report for work at 10.00 a.m. Eight minutes to kill because I planned to arrive with magnificent aplomb two minutes early. I crossed the street and moodily patrolled the perimeter of a bomb-site lit by fragile autumn sunshine. Still four minutes to go. Vaguely, as I embarked on my last introspective sortie, I became aware of a man standing on the opposite pavement gazing in my direction.

At last the moment to meet the challenge arrived. With hands clenched deep in the pockets of my lugubrious coat I re-crossed the street.

"Lambert, isn't it?"

The man I had noticed standing on the pavement regarded me curiously. He wore a well-cut raincoat and carried an umbrella; with his striped tie, gleaming black shoes and calculating features he looked the archetypal City gent. Which, unfortunately, he most certainly wasn't, as I had by now realised. His name was Kenneth Hord and he was the much-feared, much-respected news editor of the *Daily Mirror*.

Yes, I confessed, I was Lambert.

He gazed at me broodingly for a moment before demanding: "Are you short-sighted, chum?" Into that one syllable, *chum*, as I was to learn, Ken Hord could instill an octave of meaning ranging from approbation to icy rage. On this occasion the intonation wavered half way down the scale.

"No, sir," as my upper lip went into its rabbit-twitch routine. "At least I don't think so. I haven't had them tested recently. My eyes, that is. . . ."

Impatiently he interrupted the flow of faltering gibberish. "I wondered why you walked past the building three times. I thought perhaps you couldn't see it."

"Couldn't see it?" Together we gazed at the ugly great edifice in front of us and, braying like a pantomime donkey, I said: "Oh no, sir, I can see that all right."

He frowned. Myopic or not, the expression seemed to say, the new recruit was undoubtedly certifiable. "I'm glad about that, chum," he finally remarked. "Let's hope you can spot a news story a little quicker than you can spot your own office."

He turned and walked briskly towards the scruffy portals of the *Mirror* just round the corner from its present august premises.

I followed at a discreet distance arriving, contrary to my finely calculated expectations, two minutes late on my first day. Another milestone in my career to which the term chequered could only be applied in the most euphemistic sense.

*　　*　　*

It is probably difficult to comprehend the trepidation with which, at the age of twenty-three, I settled myself at an empty desk that autumn morning.

What has to be appreciated is that this was more than just a new job. Not only had I been plucked from the Provinces to the capital city, I had landed in the very citadel of journalistic flamboyance and belligerence. And I was fully aware that I had arrived at the height of the hire-and-fire era. One error of judgement and you could be feverishly looking for a new job before the rest of Fleet Street learned that you had not "res-

11

igned on a matter of principle" as you claimed: you had been booted out on your ear.

Staring across the empty, early-morning spaces of the editorial floor, with the news and picture desks becalmed in the middle, I wondered if I would find some place in the record books if I was sacked on my first day; first morning for that matter.

It was a lady named Dot Watson who helped to restore a little of my self-confidence. She was Ken Hord's secretary, a fussy, grey-haired angel of mercy, much given to emotional outbursts, who struck terror into the hearts of the typists under her wing, regarded her boss with a mixture of reverence and vexation and did her best to protect us reporters from the harsh realities of our profession.

She relieved me of my employment documents, gave me a cup of tea and a digestive biscuit, introduced me to some of my new colleagues and advised me not to be intimidated by Ken Hord's glacial air of authority.

The advice was sound, the difficulty was implementing it. Even viewed from behind, sipping his tea and scanning copy, he intimidated me. His news sense was impeccable, as was his ability to organise the coverage of a story, and it was from these foundations of meticulous efficiency that his formidable presence stemmed.

His hair was straight and on the pale side, his figure lean, his features austere. He could pluck a lie from a defensive outburst as deftly as a fielder in the slips snapping up a low catch and he looked more like an accountant than the news editor of a bristling publication such as the *Mirror*.

For six years he and his volatile intermediary, Dot Watson, were to dominate my life. But that hardly seemed likely as I sat waiting dispatch that morning to some distant theatre of war or scene of domestic mayhem.

Reporters came and went; the empty, brown-rimmed tea mugs accumulated on the desks; the hands of the clock on the wall stuttered towards midday.

Finally, the summons came, as anticlimactic as a tea-party in a brewery. Not for me escape across a crocodile-infested river to cable an exclusive; not for me a gangland shoot-out in the seedy square mile of Soho.

My assignment: to help look after a ratty little mongrel dog whom I shall call Boris and his master, a bearded tramp with a seaman's laugh and an odour of the farmyard about him, whom I shall call George.

In the early fifties much of the *Mirror's* appeal stemmed from its crusades on behalf of deprived animals. (Cats excepted because, so it was said, the chairman, Cecil King, had once confided that he rather preferred dogs to cats and this had been interpreted as an anti-moggie edict.)

A few days before my arrival at the *Mirror* a bench of country magistrates had unwisely ordered the destruction of Boris. He was, they decided, a menace to Society — and any animal within biting distance.

An alert free-lance reporter picked up the story and all over Britain there appeared newspaper headlines to the effect: KING OF THE ROAD TO BE PARTED FROM LIFE-LONG CHUM. The country rose behind Boris; there hadn't been anything quite like it since Neville Chamberlain declared war on Germany.

The *Mirror* immediately intervened, obtained a reprieve for Boris and whisked him up to London with George. Betty Tay, the animal specialist, was put in charge of the story which was to be my Fleet Street baptismal.

Betty, fortyish and attractive with a soft-spoken wit as sharp as a kitten's claw, brought pleasure to millions with her stories and weekly column of advice about pets ranging from pooches to pouter pigeons. I suspected, however, that even her infinite compassion was confounded by Boris. I sympathised with her because I, too, loved animals but, apart from his devotion to his master, Boris was decidedly short on endearing qualities.

He was a miscellany of terrier breeds; his scarred fur was dirty white and brown; his lips were frozen in a snarl and when he growled he rotated his tail in a curious manner as though it were mounted on ball-bearings.

13

Betty joined George and myself in the cramped waiting room on the editorial floor and waited until Boris had finished his ablutions. Then she said to George: "Don't worry, we'll make sure that you and your little friend are never parted again."

George tugged meditatively at his patriarchal white beard and belched. Boris began to edge, growling, towards my calf, lips tightening across his teeth.

Betty smiled hesitantly and said to me: "I suppose this isn't quite what you expected."

"Not quite," I said. Was it my imagination or had Boris's tail begun to rotate in the opposite direction?

"Don't worry," she said. "Tommy Lea will be here in a minute. He's got a way with animals."

Tommy Lea was one of the best photographers on the *Mirror's* team of cameramen. He was also a professional apologist. Before you uttered a word Tommy, small and bespectacled, would murmur: "Sorry, I didn't catch your name."

Many was the unwilling subject who had been deceived by Tommy's contrition unaware that, with every apology, his camera was clicking.

On one occasion he managed to get into the Royal Enclosure at Ascot where photography was banned. Apologising frenziedly to startled aristocracy, he managed to expose a reel of film — through a hole in his tie.

He arrived in the waiting room just as Boris had manoeuvred himself within snapping distance of my calf and apologised to everyone, even the dog. Boris sniffed his leg and rejected it with the hauteur of a wine-taster.

"Sorry about this," Tommy said, "but we'll have to take Boris outside. You know, photograph him at his best. In the open air, his natural element."

George, his voice rounded with rustic vowels, said: "I feels like a pint meself."

Betty Tay and Tommy brightened.

"But whom be going to look after Boris?" George inquired.

14

We all knew and I took the length of rope as Boris lifted his leg against the table in a valedictory gesture.

We adjourned to a Victorian pub in Fetter Lane furnished like a funeral parlour, its gloom brightened by the presence of the landlord, an Irish gnome named Barney Finnegan.

Outside Tommy Lea shook his head, a penitent about to enter the Confessional, muttered: "Sorry about this," and reached the bar in two strides.

I walked Boris up and down Fetter Lane brooding on my fate. I had weathered many vicissitudes to reach Fleet Street. To what ends? To be employed as a £20-a-week manservant walking a flea-bitten mongrel while my masters took their pleasure in a hostelry, that's what.

The day had a touch of Indian Summer about it. Weeds bloomed brightly on the bomb-sites and girls in summer frocks and blouses strode the pavements. But for me there was no distraction from my humiliating duties; not until Boris spotted a black cat on the other side of the street.

He stood for a moment rotating his tail energetically. Then he slipped his collar and was gone. A newspaper van shuddered to a halt and a workman drilling the kerb dropped his pneumatic drill and bellowed as though he had been ruptured.

The cat arched its back, spat and waited, its ferocity tempered by a trace of complacency because, according to all rules of feline-canine warfare, the dog always stopped at this juncture. Not this dog.

Boris grasped the cat's tail in his jaws and pulled like a bird tugging a worm from the ground.

My first Fleet Street assignment, menial though it was, being torn to shreds by the yellow fangs of the creature in my charge! Back to the provinces, back to funerals, motoring courts and Brixham fish prices.

I could see the headlines in the opposition newspapers. MAN FROM THE MIRROR FEEDS PUSS TO BORIS. I hurled myself across the road and kicked Boris in the rump. MAN FROM MIRROR IN SAVAGE ASSAULT ON BORIS.

The kick loosened Boris's grip on the cat which took off

across a bomb site. There were many bomb sites in the City of London in those days; exotic flowers bloomed in sun-warmed niches and the mellowing devastation was speared by jagged monuments of brick and stone, tombstones of the Blitz. There was hope, too, that enlightened architects might mould all this unsolicited space into patterns of beauty. (In most cases, of course, they utilised it to plant the foundations of grotesque monoliths.)

No time, however, for aesthetic considerations when your new job depends on you catching a dog that is chasing a cat.

Waving the rope and collar like a lasso, I stumbled across the bomb-site, tripping over tooth-stumps of brick, falling into weed-covered crevices. It was a hot day and my suit, thick and grey and all-purpose, was as heavy as a trench-coat.

"Come here Boris, old fellow," I shouted — and plunged into a shattered basement occupied by two lovers.

The man, his face contorted with thwarted passion and anger, looked up and hissed breathlessly: "My name's John, I'm not your old fellow and piss off out of here."

Fifty yards ahead the cat bounded onto the top of a ruined wall, spat and then, having established impregnability, settled down and began to lick its paws. Boris hurled himself at the wall a couple of times. Growled and rotated his tail furiously. Oddly, he never barked.

"Boris, Boris, Boris. Come here little chap."

There was really only one way for him to salvage a vestige of pride: he circled the wall slowly glancing over his shoulder to make sure that I was gaining on him, finally allowing himself to be caught with a token snarl.

I tightened the collar round his neck and returned to Fetter Lane just as Betty, Tommy and George were emerging from Barney Finnegan's.

Betty said: "Everything all right?"

"Everything's fine."

"You look very hot. You're not sickening for anything are you?"

"Rabies," I said.

16

We made our way to Lincoln's Inn Fields, seven acres of open space where newspaper photographers often took their subjects and businessmen sat on park benches munching their sandwiches and keenly observing the bouncing breasts of secretaries and typists playing net-ball.

There Tommy tried to exercise his apologetic charms on Boris. Without success. But it wasn't merely Boris's recalcitrance that defeated Tommy: it was his physical appearance.

How do you make a dog that looks like a cross between a lavatory rat and a ferret look lovable and cuddly?

Finally it was born upon us that Boris would have to be washed and beautified. Reluctantly Betty took him away in search of some miracle worker leaving Tommy and me to contemplate the net-ball players.

When Boris returned I felt sorry for him: he had been emasculated. His fur gleamed, his nails had been clipped and — the ultimate indignity — around his neck was a blue bow. He reminded me of James Cagney in drag. What's more the spirit had been knocked out of him; the sore-thumb of a tail stood erect and motionless, his teeth weren't to be seen. Happily his ugliness was undiminished. Betty removed the bow: she understood. Boris's tail rotated a couple of times in gratitude.

The problem now was two-fold: to make Boris look at the very least winsome, and to persuade George to exhibit some sort of feeling towards his lifelong chum because it had now become apparent that most of the devotion emanated from Boris.

The trick was to snap Boris in profile gazing lovingly at his master in one of the rare moments when George wasn't scratching himself. It required all the patience and ingenuity that Tommy could muster.

Boris gazed, George scratched. "Sorry," said Tommy, "we'll have to try that once again."

George stopped scratching, Boris turned his head. "Sorry," said Tommy, "just one more," the eternal cry of the Press cameraman.

By the end of the afternoon Tommy had taken dozens of

pictures and he returned to Fetter Lane to see if the picture desk art department could improve on nature. (These craftsmen were capable of removing the smile from the Mona Lisa.)

And it was then that Betty Tay pulled an unforgiveable stroke. She said with an air of martyrdom: "Well, as I'm the animal specialist I suppose I shall have to look after Boris tonight."

My spirits lifted. "No," I said without conviction, "I'll stick with him."

She shook her head. "I wouldn't dream of it."

Perhaps this was the moment when I finally lost all the innocence of youth because she smiled her gentle smile and said: "You can have George."

"I feels like a pint," George said.

"How do you mean, I can have him?"

"Look after him. Give him food and shelter. We've got another session in the morning."

I looked at George; George looked at me.

"He's a nice old chap really," Betty said.

"Do you mean put him up in a hotel?" My mind began to panic as I imagined the opening exchanges between George and the chief receptionist at the Savoy; heard George's belches reverberating round the lobby.

"I thought perhaps you could take him home. You have got a home, haven't you?"

I was renting a bed-sitter in Nottingham Place, just off Marylebone High Street, prior to finding a permanent home. The room was minute; I was 6 feet 2 inches and George was a big man; his beard, I thought, would cover both of us.

"Of course I've got a home," I said.

"Well there you are then."

"I feels like a wet," George said.

The terrible injustice of the situation was that, now that his image had been changed, Boris was docile. With a few pints inside him there was every possibility that George would become a homicidal maniac. But how could I refuse to co-operate on my first day?

18

"Have you got any money?" Betty asked.

"A couple of quid." Until pay day it was *all* I had.

"Well here's another three," she said delving into her hand-bag. "Charge it on your expenses and pay me back later." She gave the new red lead that she had bought Boris a tug. "Come on little fellow," she said.

I turned to George. "Come on big fellow," I said. "Let's go and have a jar."

George had several jars. I took him by bus to Baker Street — far away from potential humiliation in Fleet Street but close to my bed-sitter — and we started off in a pub called the Globe.

George dealt with his first pint of bitter as though it were a thimbleful of nectar. He opened his mouth and poured it down his throat without swallowing. Then pushed his empty glass towards me apparently surprised that a replacement wasn't awaiting him. The bar was crowded and this seemed to offend George, King of the Road, accustomed to supping his pint in pub gardens beneath open skies. He began to scratch vigor-ously and soon we were alone. The barman pushed George's replenished glass towards him and retreated to the other end of the bar.

George raised his glass. "'Tis a long road that has no end-ing," he said for no apparent reason and poured the second pint down his throat.

The third was taken at a more leisurely pace. Because, perhaps, George was occupied in rolling a cigarette with the contents of the dog-ends he had scooped out of the ash-tray. I sipped my half-pint and waited for some pithy anecdotes of a vagrant's life, some pearls of rustic wisdom about the migra-tion of birds, sunsets and sunrises, rings round the moon . . . I imagined George smoking a pipe with his cronies, lying in a field gazing at the stars, reminiscing about his life of freedom and independence. George nodded towards a girl at the end of the bar and said: "Got a nice bum on her, that one."

We moved to another pub where George washed down a couple of pork pies with another pint and headed for the lavatory.

19

The barmaid, classicly brassy with regulation dimpled elbows, leaned across the bar and said: "Is that your dad?"

"Good God no!"

"Dirty old devil, isn't he."

There was no answer to that. Melancholy settled upon me as I watched George emerging from the toilet in his brown jacket, probably stolen from a scarecrow, and trousers, stiff with dirt, tied above his ankles with string.

The barmaid poked me in the chest with one heavily-ringed finger. "Hey," she said, "we aren't having any of that."

"Any of what?"

"His dress."

"What about his dress?"

"He hasn't adjusted it."

Sure enough George's fly was open.

"Tell him to go back and adjust himself," the barmaid said.

I whispered to George that he had forgotten to button himself up.

George's bearded lips parted in an amiable smile. "That's right, me old darling," he said, "I likes to give the old feller an airing from time to time."

"You've got to button yourself up."

"I feels like a pint," he said.

"Well you won't get one unless you do your flies up."

"He'll have to go," the barmaid said. "It's disgusting, that's what it is."

George pushed his glass towards her.

"Get him out of here or I'll call the police."

The cynics tell us that everyone has their price and sadly they are right more often than not. I asked her if she would like a drink.

She stared at George. "Well I suppose he isn't exactly . . . you know, not exactly . . . exposed." She averted her gaze. "That's very nice of you, dearie, I'll have a large Scotch."

The bribe paid, George disposed of another pint.

We moved on to another watering hole. And then another.

By the time we reached Nottingham Place, George had downed ten pints and I had drunk seven halves and, as yet unconditioned to Fleet Street drinking habits, was feeling muddled.

The bed-sitter was in a small Georgian terrace house which accommodated six other tenants, most of whom kept detailed mental records of each other's visitors. I opened the door and crept with elaborate stealth along the passage to my room, second on the left. George rolled along behind me belching quietly into his beard.

The room contained a single bed, a small table and chair, a Belling hot-plate and a wash-basin. It seemed Lilliputian in our presence.

"You'll have to sleep on the floor," I told George; the call of duty was strong but not strong enough to allow him to use my bed.

"That's all right, me old darlin'," said George beginning to strip off. "Wouldn't sleep nowhere else."

I handed him a blanket and reached for the light-switch as he removed the first layer of newspaper wrapped round his chest. Better, I thought, never to know what lay beyond the newspaper. I undressed and lay in bed ruminating on my first day as a national newspaperman. At the very least I had anticipated an interview with a film star, Diana Dors for preference, or some dodgy City financier. Instead. . . .

Somewhere below me George made an odd snuffling noise and then began to snore — great stage snores dragged up from his socks and apparently emitted through a tin whistle. After an hour or so I slept fitfully. It was 2.30 a.m. by my illuminated wrist-watch when I heard a woman screaming.

I switched on the light. The door was open and there was no sign of George.

I put on a raincoat over my pyjamas and, looking like an archetypal Hyde Park flasher, went into the passage. Doors were opening, heads appearing. No sign of George.

Then I had an inspiration: the toilet was on the first floor. I charged up the stairs and came upon George stark naked on the landing. Standing in front of him screaming, but making no apparent effort to escape, was a middle-aged spinster in a pink dressing gown.

As I reached them George was saying: "No need for you'm to be alarmed, my pretty, I was only 'aving a tiddle."

"Christ!" I shouted at him, "couldn't you have put some clothes on?"

He looked aggrieved. "No need for you'm to get vexed matey. Me beard covers the old feller."

I lowered my gaze. George must have trimmed his beard recently.

I grabbed his arm and piloted him downstairs into my room, then rushed back to the spinster who was now wailing softly to herself. I calmed her, explained the situation and led her to her room. Either she was forgiving to a fault, or the sight of George's parts, formidable by any standards, had stunned her senses; anyway she never made a complaint and I subsequently took her to Lyon's Corner House for tea.

I smuggled George out of the house early in the morning and took him to an ABC for breakfast. It was a help-yourself service and George helped himself to everything. At the end of the counter he asked the girl at the cash desk for a paper-bag and poured the contents of the tray — bacon, sausages, buns and fruit—into it. "For a rainy day," he said, winking horribly at the astonished girl.

We caught a bus back to Fleet Street. In front of us sat two teenage girls on their way to work.

One of them was saying: "Ooh, isn't he sweet. I could just give him a great hug, couldn't you?"

"The old gentleman or the dog?" asked her companion.

"Both of them. Such a lovely little fellow, such a noble old man."

I peered over their shoulder. There, prominently displayed in the *Daily Mirror*, was a picture of George smiling fondly at Boris who, looking like the dog on the His Master's Voice record labels, was responding with a gaze of utter devotion.

II

The beauty of the reporter's lot was its unpredictability.

The shifts on the *Mirror* began at 10.00 a.m. and ended in late evening stints that got you home at dawn on a summer's morning. The early shifts were the most popular because there was always a glimmer of hope that you might be dispatched to Acapulco, or Bexhill-on-Sea for that matter; the late-night duties were the least popular because you rarely foraged farther than Hackney Marshes and the whole exercise degenerated by 4.00 a.m. into yawning boredom.

But, whatever the shift you were always an accessory to drama and every day contained the elements of a novel. An Old Bailey murder trial, an elopement to Gretna Green, a rail crash, a Teddy Boy brawl, a riot as Bill Haley and his Comets rocked around the clock. . . .

The actual mechanics of reporting were not particularly intimidating. Often it was merely the hard slog of court reporting or the tedium of door-stepping a premises on a raw winter's day to solicit a quote and receiving, instead, a thump on the ear.

As early as possible in the day you telephoned a story, then spent the rest of your sojourn writing additional material or, if developments merited it, re-jigging the introduction. You spent much of the day linked to the office by telephone, and even hot-footing it home you were enjoined to "ring in on the way, old man."

What lifted the calling above routine was the vicarious

involvement in passion and pathos, the exhileration of filling columns of newsprint with your story and knowing that millions were reading it — and the primitive excitement of pulling off an exclusive to the chagrin of your competitors.

Not that anything so ambitious came my way in those first weeks as I took my place at the reporters' desks observed speculatively by Ken Hord wondering, probably, how many sorties I had made down Fetter Lane that morning before locating the office.

*   *   *

The *Mirror* editorial floor was a great sprawling place as big as a circus arena. The reporters' desks were tucked away beside a row of green lockers on the other side of which several gorgeous secretaries with distracting bosoms lurked. In front of these desks sat Dot Watson and her assistant and in front of them the hub of the whole daily operation, the news desk.

There sat Ken Hord with, considerately, his back to us and, separated by trays of copy, spikes and mugs of tea, his assistants sifting stories as they came off typewriter and teleprinter and answering the batteries of incessantly-ringing telephones.

Away to the left sat the picture editor with his team dispatching cameramen on assignments and studying the pictures flooding into the office from agencies, free-lances and staffmen. Beyond the news and picture desks stood the back bench where the night executives reigned and the sub-editors' desks where copy was clipped, polished, corrected and slotted snugly into its allotted space somewhere in a seven-column tabloid page.

As the day accelerated those reporters without a job — their numbers swelled by in-coming shifts — began to twitch a bit, leaping clumsily to their feet when their name was finally called. A summons from Ken Hord, or his second-in-command, the smooth and capable Cliff Pearson, meant a story that at least stood some chance of getting into the paper; a call from one of the assistants probably meant phoning a

24

ministry for a quote or interviewing an informant in the tiny waiting room where I had first been introduced to George and Boris.

While we waited the stars swept past the desks. Bill Connor, the dumpy bespectacled author of the Cassandra column whose torrential output and rumbustious wit has never been equalled; Noel Whitcomb, a columnist who could convert a tumbler of Lucozade into a glass of champagne in a housewife's hand; and lordly visitors from overseas such as Ralph Champion, talent-scouting for his bureau in New York. His perceptive gaze always slid hastily over my thick-suited figure topped by a head of hair that always looked as though I had just emerged from a Dublin bar brawl.

Occasionally the editor, Jack Nener, who wore shirts as snowy white as his hair, would explode into the news room as though propelled by his bow-tie. If ever a man looked like an editor it was Jack Nener. Sometimes Hugh Cudlipp, the leonine Welsh wizard who directed operations, would materialise and an unnatural hush would descend on the place.

The truly electric moments occurred when a big story broke. Ken Hord wheeled round in his chair and barked out the names of the chosen few. Perhaps it was an out-of-town murder, the best type of assignment in an era when sudden and mysterious death was even more addictive reading than it is today, preferably a poisoning with midnight exhumations and exhaustive inquiries which could continue for weeks and *Entertaining contacts* could be worth three or four quid a day.

Crime reporters and photographers, collectively a most secretive breed of journalists, assembled while the chauffeur-driven Humber Hawks waited in the courtyard, engines ticking over. (Few journalists possessed cars and Anne Lloyd-Williams was regarded as a plutocrat when she bought a black Ford Popular.) Then they were all gone and one man was left to try and stitch together a makeshift early story on the telephone.

By the time I had been left to carry out this task for the third or fourth time I knew the form: Clippings from the library in case the victim was famous or infamous; a potted biography on the detective in charge of the case — Bert Hannam, say, or Jack (Softly, Softly catchee monkey) Capstick. Maps and reference books. Phone calls to the nearest pub, newsagents and neighbours, their names culled from an electoral guide. And, in those pre-Press Council days, a call to the home of the corpse, where, if your star was in the ascent, you might extract some nugget of information.

Lastly a call to the local police station where a desk sergeant would wearily intone: "All inquiries are being referred to the Press Bureau at Scotland Yard", an attitude which was only varied when the police wanted help from the Press. The advice was, in any case, superfluous because every national paper had a man at the Yard, in the *Mirror's* case Jeep Whittall, the only teetotal reporter I ever met.

If the story was really big and time was pushing on the chief-sub sometimes circumvented the news desk by snatching the top copy of the first page from your typewriter because, in those days, the first editions for the North Country went to press very early in the evening. Editions were designated by stars under the red-lettered title DAILY MIRROR and the slogan FORWARD WITH THE PEOPLE, the biggest number of copies being the one-star. The last editions when front and back pages were miraculously re-jigged for late-breaking stories were devoid of stars.

Because of the problem of these early editions — a problem not shared by such papers as the *Express* or *Mail* which printed in Manchester — I sometimes saw my early copy in print; but it was soon ejected by stories telephoned by the men on the spot.

Activity in the newsroom reached a crescendo in the evening as the last pages for the early editions were put together; elsewhere slugs of hot metal type were being slotted by compositors into the spaces between advertising and photographic blocks and converted into moulds which were clamped round the great rotary presses spewing out millions of copies of the paper.

Away went the papers in vans driven by Kamakazi drivers to railway stations and airports, tied in great bundles with coarse string, accompanied by posters to help sell them in the morning.

By about 9.00 a.m. the editorial floor was relatively calm and the barking voices of the night executives could plainly be heard. The night editor was a mercurial, dark-haired genius named Dick Dinsdale who, when offended by some glaring inadequacy in a story, would hold up the copy by one corner as though it were a soiled handkerchief and thunder: "Well, piss on my yellow boots." So often did he extend this invitation that I used to furtively examine his footwear; disappointingly they were always shiny, black and dry.

On one such night the deputy night news editor, John Theobald, who managed to combine desk-bound efficiency with swash-buckling airs, handed me a sheaf of copy from agencies and correspondents, the weather story, the nadir of journalistic endeavour.

Secret knowledge was printed on his piratical features. "You have been honoured," he told me.

"I have?"

I glanced at the pages of copy. Jam-packed roads, bumper-to-bumper traffic, sizzling beaches — the formula which generations of reporters had tried in vain to change. The honour was not apparent.

"Ever had a by-line, lad?"

I shook my head. I hadn't yet been in remote contact with any story that merited my name on it.

He held up his hand. "Wait for it."

I waited.

"You are to be the first *Daily Mirror Weathercock*."

And indeed I was. And for a brief period that accreditation appeared on top of every *Mirror* weather report.

When I got home that night - we had by this time found a flat in Richmond - my wife said: "Well, how did it go?" steadying herself to absorb my daily litany of despair.

"You're a lucky woman," I said.

27

"Lucky?"

"Honoured."

"You mean you've got a rise?"

"Not quite. But in future you will be able to hold your head high and tell you friends that you are married to the first *Daily Mirror Weathercock*."

But by far the most formidable of the nocturnal executives was Ted Castle, the night picture editor and husband of politician Barbara Castle. Ted was a fierce looking fellow whose rasping, platform-speaker's voice would have dispatched the most mutinous of troops Over the Top.

He once barked a series of orders at a particularly timorous freelance photographer.

The photographer backed away not having understood a word he had said. "But Ted. . ." he began.

"Don't hang about, just get there man."

Unhappily the photographer picked up his heavy camera case. He was a small man and it almost dislocated his shoulder.

"But Ted. . ."

"On your way man, for pity's sake."

The photographer slunk away not having the slightest idea where he was supposed to go.

He gave it five minutes and then called Ted Castle from the house phone at the bottom of the stairs.

Ted snatched up the expension. "Picture desk."

"Ted, it's me."

"Who the devil's me?"

The photographer gave his name.

"Are you on your way?"

"Yes, but. . ."

"Call me when you get there," Ted snapped and hung up.

The photographer stumbled along Fetter Lane to Barney Finnegan's. A glittering future on the *Mirror* extinguished by faint-heart. Mortgages to pay, little mouths to feed. . . .

Half an hour later he called the picture desk fortified against the final humiliation by several large whiskies.

"Picture desk," snapped Ted.

"Ted, it's me."

"Ah. Have you got there?"

"Yes," said the photographer deciding to bring down the curtain on the farce with a touch of irony.

"Good man," said Ted crisply. "But there's nothing in it. Get back to the office as fast as you can."

Sadly Ted, later Lord Castle, died while I was writing this book. I think he would have enjoyed the story.

*   *   *

During various lulls in the evening reporters and subs slipped away to their chosen pubs. Reporters in their interview-suits, subs in their gardening clothes. They didn't mix a lot over their pints because each breed favoured a particular hostelry — and there were enough to go round in the side streets and alleyways between Holborn and Fleet Street.

Barney Finnegan's apart, the other most popular pub in Fetter Lane was No. 10, run by a stout lady named Winnie. But this was used mostly be executives and raffish staffmen from the *Sunday Pictorial,* the *Mirror's* stable-mate.

If a journalist from another national newspaper was spotted in a *Mirror* pub then, within minutes, word had vaulted the bars along the length of Fleet Street that he was looking for a job on the *Mirror*; likewise if a *Mirror* man was seen skulking in Poppins he was after a job on the *Express*; if he was in the Harrow then his target was the *Mail*.

The most traumatic moment of the evening for those taking a break in Barney Finnegan's was 10.25 p.m. Should we get in another round or belt round the corner to the Blue Anchor which, being in another borough, didn't close until eleven?

Most of us opted for the Blue Anchor where we were received under sufferance and the refined ladies behind the bar were heard to murmur: "Let the buggers wait." And wait we did while pints were pulled with histrionic flourishes for the regulars who had been lodged there since opening time.

Frequently we were recalled by telephone to the newsroom

before we had got our order in and we returned abjectly like terminally sick patients deprived of a wonder drug.

Pints of bitter and bottles of Guinness were the favourite tipples. Anyone ordering a short must have pulled an expenses coup; anyone ordering a glass of wine in those days was a pouf.

By the time we got back from the Anchor the Back Bench and news desk were scanning the early editions of the opposition as feverishly as punters checking their football pools. If an exclusive was splashed across a front page then we were given the thankless task of trying to confirm it; thankless because, if the story was that good, then the protagonists had invariably been whisked away to some unlikely hotel guarded by the Hairy-arsed Mob as a paper's more muscular reporters were known.

On occasions a member of the hotel staff would earn himself a fiver by phoning us and revealing the whereabouts of the quarry. The ensuing fracas was memorable. If the personalities involved in the exclusive had been left in their rooms by an over-confident guard then it was sometimes possible to reach them. They had usually been paid and warned not to communicate with rival newspapers. But they were often bewildered and unaware how a few non-committal replies could be converted into publishable copy.

Even the most innocuous remark could be extended into:

Runaway vicar Joe Bloggs, aged 98, last night talked about his relationship with his verger's 17-year-old daughter.

Silver-haired Bloggs, married for 60 years to the childhood sweetheart whom he met at Sunday school, stood at a bedroom door in a plush honeymoon hotel and said: "I've been told not to say anything."

Midway through such an interview the unwary bodyguard would return and thrust the protesting vicar back into the bedroom. A punch-up would then ensue.

Result: Everyone would be thrown out of the hotel enabling the *Mirror* photographer to snatch flashlight photographs of the vicar and a pert seventeen-year-old blonde being bundled unceremoniously into a waiting limousine.

Next morning the executives of the rival newspaper would rage impotently and the unfortunate guard would be fired or relegated to up-dating obituaries.

Of course it could work the other way round when some mercenary night porter tipped off the opposition about a *Mirror* exclusive.

The other phenomenon arising from the early editions was the Transfer Syndrome. This occurred when the night editor of, say, the *Express* admired the *Mirror's* choice of story for the lead on the front page; equally the night editor of the *Mirror* admired the *Express's* selection. In the later editions the *Mirror* would lead the paper with the *Express* story and vice versa.

By the early hours of the morning, after the big edition had gone, there was a marked decrease in the tempo of activity. The expanses of empty, green-topped desks looked seedy — like a beach after an August Bank Holiday — their surfaces littered with the day's dropping. Empty cups, greasy plates, toppled spikes, overflowing ash-trays, wet proofs now dried and crinkled. The floor was papered with discarded copy and early editions.

The atmosphere of desolate exhaustion grew bleaker as the last journalists departed for home or the Press Club leaving behind the late-night sub, the late-duty reporter and a desk-man named Issy Pitman whose job was to meld night and day.

Issy had been around for a long time. His hair and moustache were silver-grey and he looked like a distinguished diplomat, Anthony Eden without that Bugs Bunny look. Issy talked incessantly, answered the occasional telephone calls from drunks and informants, crediting the latter with 10s.6d. if they were the first to report a crash, a knifing, or a fire . . . fires only made the paper if they were Raging Infernoes but the credit was dispatched in the belief that, if one day the inform-ant saw a cat-burglar climbing the walls of Buckingham Palace, he would ring the *Mirror* first. A small neat item taken by the last remaining copy-taker was always welcome at this time because the late-night sub could squeeze it into the fudge, or Stop Press as the blank space is better known.

31

If a really big story broke and it merited the cost of re-jigging the paper, the office became dramatically re-animated, as though a bank shoot-out sequence had suddenly been inserted into a dreamy travelogue. Reporters, subs and executives were yanked out of the Press Club. Phones jangled, typewriters clattered, orders were yelled.

When the smoke had cleared only Issy Pitman remained. Calmly perusing *The Times* for possible stories in the small ads, composing his report for the day men.

Just before dawn the cleaners burst into Issy's cocoon of tranquillity. Plump ladies using their mops like hockey sticks and loudly discussing their husbands' iniquities. Majestically, Issy gathered together his papers and retired to the managing editor's office. When he re-emerged the after-birth of publication had been removed and the newsroom was ready for the daily re-birth. The first day desk-man arrived stretching and yawning; Issy handed over and retired to his bed in Highgate. The telephone rang: the first hesitant pangs of labour had begun. . . .

When Issy had a day off one of the general news reporters were detailed to do his shift. One such reporter was sipping his 7.00 a.m. mug of tea when first reports of a train crash began to filter through. He called the news and picture editors, frantically grabbing at telephone extensions as they jangled around him. He duly accredited the first informant and, in the circumstances, one or two more.

Finally his control broke. "I suppose," he sneered into a telephone, "you're another ghoul wanting his half guinea."

There was a pause. Then a voice said: "As a matter of fact I'm not. This is the editor speaking."

III

The *Mirror* reporters were a wildly assorted bunch, not one of them bearing any resemblance to the public conception of a Fleet Street scribe.

Hugh Saker, for instance, with his one good eye and one glass one and magnificent belly as taut as a base drum; Peter Woods, a charcoal-grey-suited giant with a Gentleman's Relish voice who now reads the news on BBC television; Harry Longmuir, a Scot with pleasantly crumpled features who moved to the *Daily Mail* to become one of the country's top investigative journalists; the exuberant Desmond Wilcox completing a stint in New York before settling down with the BBC and subsequently marrying Esther Rantzen; Howard Johnson, the chief reporter and one of God's gentlemen. . . .

But the most formidable of the pack were the ladies led in physical stature and aggressive personality by an Australian named Liz Hickson, who achieved immortality by pouring a cup of tea over an executive's head. She was blonde and buxom and inexorable in pursuit of a story; when an exhausted quarry finally surrendered she would try to wheedle quotes from his trembling lips; if this failed then, I suspected, she gave him a good whack round the head with her handbag. Her expense accounts were legendary but she gave the *Mirror* good value.

Anne Lloyd - Williams' approach was different; femininity and sympathy were her stock in trade. She was the daughter of a chief constable and, such was her impeccable style, that she soon became Court reporter, accompanying the Queen and the Duke of Edinburgh on all their tours.

The complement was made up by Mary Malone, a lissom colleen with the figure of a fashion model: she had no difficulty whatsoever in interviewing the most recalcitrant of males because they all fell in love with her.

But male or female, extrovert or introvert, suave or belligerently forthright, none of the reporters was adverse to the rough and tumble of adventure in the field, in particular the chases.

These were often spectacular and hair-raising, especially when a newspaper had exclusive access to a protagonist in a story. If the *Mirror* had someone in tow then I often acted as bodyguard and decoy. If we were traced to an hotel then I would take off in a limousine at great pace accompanied by figures shrouded in blankets.

Dispatch riders on motor cycles, used on these occasions because they were difficult to shake off, would roar off in pursuit while the office driver, always game for Keystone Cops stuff, would put his foot down, take corners on two wheels, shoot traffic lights on the red and weave across the road grinning fiendishly if he managed to edge a motor-cyclist into a ditch.

Behind the dispatch-riders came the rival newspapers' office cars. Finally we would allow ourselves to be cornered and out would step our companions divested of their blankets, two chambermaids and the night porter from the hotel.

The most spectacular chases took place during the romance between Princess Margaret and Group Captain Peter Townsend. All the world's Press was involved, *Paris-Match* and the rest of the French to the fore.

The story had actually been broken in Britain way back in 1952 by the Sunday newspaper, the *People*. And as far as the public was concerned it had everything: a handsome commoner, Battle of Britain hero and former equerry to the late King George VI courting the Queen's sister.

The Wicked Baron was the Establishment which predictably reacted with refined hysteria at the prospect of such a match because there *was* a flaw to the romantic ideal: the Group Captain, cousin of the Labour leader, Hugh Gaitskell, had been divorced.

Princess Margaret was at the time twenty-three. Two years to wait before she was free of a clause of the Royal Marriage Act of 1772 which forbade her to marry without the Queen's consent before the age of twenty-five.

Separation was the obvious solution. Princess Margaret was fortuitously about to embark on a visit to Rhodesia with her mother; Townsend was dispatched to Brussels to become air attaché to the British Embassy two days before the Princess was due to return.

Throughout the saga the Wicked Baron, as far as the media was concerned, was the Queen's Press Secretary, Commander Richard Colville, a severe gentleman who favoured black clothes and was temperamentally far better suited to his former occupation — paymaster in the Royal Navy.

In retrospect he wasn't all that wicked. Merely misplaced. Acknowledging only good news and therefore ludicruously non-committal about the bad. Treating Royalty with Victorian reverence in an age when the Monarchy was finding the common touch. Handling the naturally inquisitive Press — they represented an insatiably curious Public — as though they were Peeping Toms.

According to Townsend himself in his memoirs public relations reached such a pitch of asininity that Colville's office once denied that the post of Comptroller to the Queen Mother — the job which the Queen Mother had herself asked him to accept after her husband's death — had ever existed. Had communications with the Press been more openly handled then some of the wilder excesses of speculation might have been avoided. But so, too, would the thrills of the chase.

For a while, however, the story faded while Townsend served out his exile in Brussels. Although he did once hop into England and, unknown to the newspapers, spend a couple of hours with the "Dolly Princess."

The story erupted once more in Brussels before the final explosion in Britain after the Princess's twenty-fifth birthday. By the time Townsend arrived back in London she had been told that, if she went through with the marriage, she would have to renounce all Royal privileges, including income. Townsend was pursued all the way from the air terminal at Lydd to a flat in Knightsbridge by a Keystone Cops squad of Pressmen. The Siege of Lowndes Square had began.

It was staged for twenty-four hours a day and it lasted for two weeks. While the Church, Cabinet and Privy Council loftily debated the embarrassing affair, we hard newsmen camped out on the square recording every visit, surging frantically forward when Townsend emerged from the building, hurling ourselves into office cars to take up the chase again when he drove off.

He took us to Clarence House where the Queen Mother lived. He took us to Binfield in Berkshire. He took us to Uckfield in Sussex. We crashed cars, pushed out-riders into ditches, snatched pictures, corrupted servants of stately homes who looked mortified if we didn't make at least a token assault on their moral turpitude. Meanwhile back at THE BUILDINGS, Colville excelled himself by officially announcing that no announcement was at present contemplated.

And so the chases went on as Peter and his Princess continued to meet. And most of us got the impression that, although he didn't relish the role of quarry, Townsend compared us favourably with the pained PRO's at the Palace who had never once come to his aid. Harrassed though he was, he was always pleasant. And on the few occasions that we lost him we got the impression that he slowed down a bit to give us time to catch up. Why not? At least we were his friends.

Finally the story drew to its long-overdue climax. The power to stop the marriage had now passed from the Queen to Parliament and the governments of the seven dominions.

Doubtless they would have given reluctant approval provided the Princess relinquished all Royal rights. But such a sacrifice was too great to expect her to make. She was, after all, aware of the oblivion to which the Duke and Duchess of Windsor had been dispatched. She issued a statement that she had decided to honour her duty to the Commonwealth and respect the Church's teaching that Christian marriage was indissoluble.

Bar last knockings, the story was over. For me the coverage of the ill-starred romance had been a salutory experience: I had been on the fringe of a world-wide news story and I hadn't disgraced myself. (No one was aware that on one occasion I had overtaken the car that Townsend was driving.)

What's more I had discovered the cameraderie which accompanies rivalry between newspapermen. And I had discovered the world of the small hotel. . . .

*   *   *

Hotel managers, like the public for that matter, were unequivocal in their attitude to Pressmen: they either loved or loathed them. If, as newspapermen descended onto their territory, hoteliers immediately hung out NO VACANCIES signs we decided that they had something to hide. ("What have you got to hide?" was a favourite question in the presence of a particularly obdurate subject who, if he had any sense at all, declined to answer either in the affirmative or negative.)

Those who loved us kept the bar open all night, served cheese sandwiches around the clock, took our telephone calls, lied to newsdesks about our whereabouts and generally entered into the spirit of the story.

In the morning they scanned all the newspapers and would toss the *Daily Mail* on the breakfast table and observe with brutal *bon homie*: "See Rodney pulled one on you yesterday," which was often only too true if Rodney Hallworth had been on the story, or wave the *Express* across the eggs and bacon to display an exclusive by Percy Hoskins or Don Seaman. Or "Didn't see anything from you, Derek," as I pushed aside my kippers untouched.

Their rewards for this participation were the anecdotal

37

entertainment which most Pressmen can magically produce at the first sip of a pint — and astronomic bar profits which enabled them to take off for the South of France as soon as we had departed.

I only saw one such manager falter in his geniality and that was when he finally went to lock up and discovered a diminutive cameraman from the *Evening Standard* named Billy Breeze suspended by his braces from a hat-stand in the hall. He lifted him off and brushed him down whereupon Billy blinked sleepily and said: "How about one for the road, governor?"

*   *   *

But, Townsend apart, out-of-town stories rarely came my way. Bow Street Magistrates Court, occasionally the Law Courts or the Old Bailey, was usually the limit of my excursions, always accompanied by the spectre of failure.

The stories with which I was trusted were of the variety that "just might make it" and often I had to call the news desk with the dreaded phrase: "It doesn't stand up." This statement was always greeted with stunned incredulity as though I were responsible for not injecting newsworthy ingredients into the tale.

"Are you sure old boy?"

(We were always "old boy" or "old man.")

"I'm afraid so."

"But it had all the makings, old man."

"I know it did but the woman in question was on the game."

A pause while the instigator of the story hesitated to consider the effect of the lady's profession on a story of blighted romance.

"Are you sure?"

"Well she was fined two quid for soliciting."

"Ah."

Another pause.

"I suppose. . ."

"She had fifteen previous convictions."

A sigh. "Better get back then, old man," in a tone that implied I had put the girl on the road to ruin.

They were bleak places those lower courts presided over by a stipendary magistrate — although the author of *Courts Day by Day*, the column in the *Evening News*, managed to instil humour and compassion into them — and they smelled of Mansion Polish and faintly of prison.

First the jetsam of the night before. The drunks, vagrants and the whores who were dealt with by the magistrates as swiftly as bookies calling out the odds.

"How do you. . ."

"Guilty."

"Fined five pounds."

"Time to pay?"

"One month. Next case."

And into the dock with a swagger and a swing of her hips would step another slit-skirted beauty fluttering eyelashes as big as butterflies and whispering audibly to an embarrassed young policeman: "I can squeeze you in for a quickie this afternoon, George."

Then there would be the attempted suicides, compulsive shop-lifters and drug addicts; and suddenly you saw them as they might have been when they were children. . . .

If you were lucky a story fell into your lap while you were waiting for your case. As it did when a man named Smith appeared charged with indecent exposure in Green Park. It so happened that this particular Smith was the husband of a famous but faded Society beauty.

He stood in the dock, tall and thin with a prominent Adam's Apple and cadaverous features, looking like an underpaid clerk from a Dickensian solicitor's office. What made the case different was that he had exposed himself to delectable secretaries taking the sunshine in their lunch-hour by raising his bowler hat.

Even the magistrate who had heard most things was taken by surprise.

"He did what?"

The policeman stared at his feet and muttered: "Exposed himself by raising his bowler hat."

The police inspector sitting in the well of the court looked worried: no one had told him that one of his constables had gone off his head.

The magistrate, a man who managed to combine kindliness with his own brand of bored arrogance, gazed at the policeman in wonderment. "Pray explain yourself, officer."

The policeman clenched his fists and stared at a spot somewhere above the magistrate's head. "He sat on a park bench, with his bowler hat on his . . . his . . ."

"On his knees?"

"A bit above, your honour."

"Ah," understanding beginning to dawn.

"And whenever a young lady passed by he lifted his bowler hat and said 'Good afternoon miss.' "

"Good grief," said the magistrate; and then, involuntarily, "What did they reply?"

"Only one did, sir."

"And what did she say, pray?"

"Good afternoon Mr. Thomas," said the policeman grimacing horribly.

The magistrate sat back in his chair. He was a man revived: he who had believed that nothing new could materialise before his cynical gaze had been confounded. But there was more to come.

Unhappily, the solicitor for the defence, precise and pinstriped, rose to his feet.

"You see, your honour, the defendant has this weakness." A pause. "It has to do with his . . . ah . . . bladder."

"You mean he's incontinent?"

It really only needed someone to ask how he could have been exposing himself in Green Park if he was on the Continent. . . .

"Exactly," said the solicitor wishing that he had remembered the word.

40

"Please get to the point," the magistrate said.

"Well with this condition he has to take certain precautions." The solicitor closed his eyes. "You see it's not really a bowler-hat it's a re-enforced chamber-pot."

Mr. Smith was conditionally discharged.

*　　*　　*

Because of its rapport with its readers, the *Mirror* also extended my limited knowledge of the human race beyond malfunctioning bladders. For three years I had been too busy improving myself to stand back and observe; now I suddenly made the belated discovery that ordinary people did not exist; that behind every door on which I knocked there existed self-contained drama.

In particular I discovered the pride and pathos that are the adjunct of so many swaggering headlines. The bully-boy in the dock sneering at the judge who had dispatched him to jail for five years; his hopeless wife pretending to her children that he'd gone to sea.

The Teddy Boy who knifed a rival to death on Clapham Common; the bewildered, hard-working parents of both boys wondering where they had gone wrong.

The legacy of desolate grief left by a suicide; the quiet devotion of parents towards a crippled child; barely-noticed acts of heroism at scenes of disaster; the inarticulate intensity of teenage infatuation; the defiant loneliness of old people isolated in cacophonous blocks of flats. . . .

It was more the *Mirror's* understanding of these facets of the human condition than their coverage of the exploits of the famous and privileged that was responsible for their circulation that was bounding towards the magic five million. (In fact the knowledgeable claimed that this figure was uneconomic.) And it was up to us to unearth these facets.

A football pools win, for instance. A Mr. William Tull won £27,000 for 6d on the treble chance. I was given the story because, although it wasn't the sort of fortune that merited a presentation by a film star, it "just might make".

I went to Church Path, Acton Green, to interview Mr. Tull, who was eighty-one, and discovered that, throughout his fifty-two years of married life he had, unknown to his wife, placed a bet every week. Ever since the end of World War II he had also secretly blown 2s. a week on the pools. The Tulls were never far from the poverty line and each time he filled in his coupon he had prayed that the investment would "bring a nest-egg for my Ada."

Finally it had. Too late. Ada, aged eighty-two, was bedridden and blind. All he could do with the money was buy a white-washed cottage somewhere amid green fields. A bright new home that she would never see. Ironically this sad little tale brought me a dividend. My first by-line in the *Mirror*. HIS £27,000 LUCK IS TOO LATE and underneath *By Derek Lambert*.

Throughout the next day I read and re-read the story sandwiched between a picture of the Duke of Edinburgh sniffing a glass of beer at the Brewing Industry Research Foundation and an advertisement for Chef Tomato Ketchup, price 1s. 3d. It is probably difficult for the layman to appreciate the delirious joy that this small achievement ignited. And indeed there are many reporters who minimise the value of by-lines — usually those who don't get too many of them.

Some time during the day Ken Hord paused beside my desk and murmured: "Well done, chum," while Dot Watson executed a thumbs-up behind his back.

I had arrived — thanks to Mr. William Tull and his weekly flutter.

IV

Newspaper photographers can, generally speaking, be divided into two schools: hard news and features.

Each regards the other with a certain amount of disdain. The hard news cameraman dismisses the feature specialist as an effete amateur and attributes any of his special effects to camera wobble or bad focussing; the features photographer regards the hard news man as a happy snapper who would be just as gainfully employed on Blackpool seafront.

But there are a talented few who can turn their hands to any assignment and it is these adaptable professionals who annually clean up the awards where several categories of pictures have to be submitted.

Freddie Reed was the star of the *Mirror* team, a highly-strung perfectionist, without whom, one suspected, the Queen and the Duke of Edinburgh would have been reluctant to depart on a Royal tour. The other stars were George Greenwell, Bela Zola and Tommy Lea who, when dispatched to the London Zoo, was purportedly heard apologising to the animals for invading their privacy.

But it was the crime photographers, confirming more to the popular conception of newspapermen, who always guaranteed a lively assignment.

The relationship between reporter and photographer was always fraught. The photographer believed that the reporter had been sent to write a caption for his picture: the reporter believed the cameraman had been sent to illustrate his story.

The relationship frequently disintegrated when a reporter

described an incident that the photographer claimed had never happened and therefore could not be photographed, or when the reporter got in front of the camera at the critical moment.

The alert reporter realised that the cameraman had only one chance and got out of his way. If, for instance, some sanctimonious villain had previously indicated his reluctance to be interviewed, you then knocked on his front door and leaped aside while the cameraman photographed an irate face, often accompanied by a bunched fist, framed in the doorway.

Photographers were not always quite so charitable in their attitude to us scribes.

I was once standing outside the Law Courts chatting to a lawyer trying to extract a modicum of information from him. He was a very elegant young man wearing striped trousers and an exaggerated expression of disdain. The conversation was tortuous but I thought I was getting through to him by complimenting him on his defence of some ageing abortionist.

"She'd be inside now if it wasn't for you," I said.

"Do you really think so, *Mirror*?" filtering a laugh through his front teeth.

"Damn right I do. Your command of the English language is absolutely prodigious."

·"The old Varsity touch, I suppose. What, what?"

"It must be," lowering my voice in shame. "I didn't have that advantage."

"Nothing like it *Mirror*.

"Of course not." Now for the question — the whereabouts of a particular witness in a case in which he was appearing. "I wonder . . ."

At that moment a photographer not renowned for a sophisticated approach to his duties materialised in front of us.

The lawyer backed nervously away whereupon the photographer cocked one leg, let go a thunderous fart, slapped him on the back, bawled: "Dirty bastard," and went on his way.

The address of the witness was never revealed.

The incident was only surpassed in my experience during an interview with a church dignitary who had just returned from a visit to South Africa. Also present was a photographer, also rather less than urbane.

The exchanges had proceeded at a suitably genteel pace in the Primate's sitting-room overlooking the cloisters. Pigeons cooed on the balcony, somewhere we could hear the splashing of a fountain. Gently, I attempted to ease some controversial opinion from the benign, white-haired man of God. Without much luck.

His wife served tea and biscuits. We sipped and munched and regarded each other tranquilly across a rosewood table. Then the cleric became sorry for the grizzled photographer who had so far contributed little towards the conversation beyond a request for five lumps of sugar in his tea.

He smiled at the cameraman stirring his sugar-stiff potion and inquired: "And what do you think about apartheid?"

The photographer frowned as though confronted with the 50,000 dollar question on an American TV quiz game.

We waited.

Finally he put down his cup, stared intently at the good churchman and said: "Well, your lordliness, in my opinion it all depends on the size of your chopper."

*   *   *

Most of the popular papers employed, in addition to crime photographers, contact men popularly known as picture snatchers. They were a plausible, raffish clan who spent much of their time drinking with policemen and commanded phenomenal expenses. Their job was to liase with the C.I.D. and the villains in a story and to lay their hands on as many photographs as possible.

And snatch pictures they occasionally did. In fact it was not unknown for a picture of Aunt Edna with the children to be swiped off a mantelpiece while a reporter was deep in conversation with the occupant of a house, copied outside the premises and returned to the mantelpiece without the owner missing it.

45

The *Mirror's* contact man was Sid Brock who looked more like a detective superintendent than anyone at Scotland Yard. He was stockily built, wore starched white collars, smoked a pipe and conversed in police jargon.

He was one of the more responsible contact men who didn't *nick* pictures, and, in fact, it was a paradox of the *Mirror*, as bold and brash as a Cockney barmaid, that many of its employees were reserved and austere. Ken Hord, for instance, and his night counterpart, Mike Anderson, who gave the impression that he had just left the lectern or pulpit.

Much of the picture snatchers' endeavours — indeed the endeavours of the whole crime team — were directed towards gathering background of such an incriminating nature that it could only be used after a defendant had been convicted and sentenced. Frequently months of sinister application was wasted when the man in the dock was acquitted and the indignation of the journalists was only equalled by the fury of the police.

The suspense became acute when the defendant was convicted late in the evening and the judge postponed sentence until the following day. To publish or not to publish? Strictly speaking the publication of background material constituted contempt of court; on the other hand the jury had made their decision and couldn't be influenced and no judge would be influenced by the assertion that a school-teacher had possessed homicidal tendencies when he was eight years old.

The problem was referred to the office lawyers who read all copy that could possibly involve litigation. The grief of the journalist whose background was killed by the lawyers was terrible to behold, especially if another paper's legal experts permitted the story to be published — although frequently such a cavalier approach landed them in deep trouble.

The main problem facing crime photographers was the law prohibiting photography within the environs of the court; the trouble was that no one had clearly defined *environs*. Pictures would normally be taken as a defendant or witness walked blinking into the daylight, but if a judge had complained then the environs had to be expanded.

Photographers would leap from behind parked cars or, in the case of the Old Bailey, a tea-shop across the road. The best course of action for the quarry was to co-operate and get it over with otherwise he would be pursued with organised cunning.

Just when he thought he had shaken off the hounds a man in a bulky overcoat, hat on the back of his head, cigarette attached to his lower lip, would detach himself from a pillar at Waterloo and bang! The station would explode with flashlight.

If he successfully managed evasive action then they got him at home. "Excuse me sir," as he slid the key into the lock. As he turned involuntarily a Speed-Graphic plate camera appeared above the privet hedge and bang. . . .

If by this time anyone should be feeling sorry for the quarry it should be remembered that frequently they were wealthy citizens to whom a fine was a minor inconvenience: the punishment that hurt was the publicity.

*   *   *

One of the first big crime stories I covered ended on a farcical and, for me, potentially disastrous note.

A woman had been stabbed to death with a Scout knife in Bournemouth. In common with Eastbourne and Torquay this resort possessed intrinsic qualities beneficial to such a story: violent death had much more impact among palm trees and wheel-chairs than it did in the seedy confines of Soho.

The Press booked into the best hotel they could find and, after phoning an early and adequate story, the reporters went out to play. It was high summer; the beer was warm, the sea breezes cool and the town swarming with pretty girls, pink, peeling or done to a turn.

When toiling on the *Dartmouth Chronicle* and studying any book I could lay my hands on about Fleet Street I once read that Pressmen were so dedicated to their jobs that they weren't interested in sex. I found this information disturbing and for a while my resolve wavered; however subsequent experience made me suspect that the author must have had some unfortunate operation.

That night we supped a few ales, made the obligatory mysterious phone calls designed to keep the opposition on their toes and adjourned to a dance-hall because it had an extension of drinking hours.

Dance stylists were swooping round the floor as though it were a skating rink, spinning and bending at the knee or trying to break their partners' backs in the tango. I watched all this moodily because I had never excelled on the dance floor. In my teens I had gone to the Hammersmith Palais or Lyceum and, after a couple of light ales, steeled myself for a Palais Glide or the last waltz.

Conversation was always tortuous. "Do you come here often?"

"Yes."

"Do you live on the Number eleven bus route?"

"No."

The exchanges occasionally relieved by an apology from the girl when I kicked her on the shin.

Uniforms, particularly American ones, were the secret of success but my A.T.C. best-blues — the trousers a different shade of blue to the jacket — didn't seem to have much pull. I was finally put to flight when I asked a girl to dance and she said: "No thanks I'm sweating."

In the Bournemouth dance-hall a girl actually asked me to dance. She was blonde and curvaceous and smelled of strawberries. We took to the floor while my colleagues winked, leered and drank my beer.

My joints were oiled with ale and for once I danced with confidence only vaguely aware of other couples leaping out of the way. Not only that but I was articulate and voluble and talk turned to the murder as I executed a tricky turn catching one of the stylists a glancing blow with my elbow.

48

"They've got the murder weapon," I confided.

We had moved into the *Moonlight Serenade*. Other couples were whispering to each other and embracing dreamily. I persevered with homicide.

"It must have been someone she trusted," I said.

"Who?"

"The dead woman."

"Ah."

"She let him into the house."

"Really?"

I nodded authoritatively, pirouetted and knocked a glass of beer off a table. After the dance I took her back to her seat and returned to my colleagues.

Ten minutes later a man wearing a brown suit and heavy-duty shoes tapped me on the shoulder and said: "Excuse me, sir, would you come outside a minute."

"Who are you?" I asked as the bounce and swagger drained away.

"A police officer."

Outside he said: "We'd be obliged if you would accompany us to the police station."

"Why, for God's sake?"

"You were dancing with a young lady a few minutes ago?"

"Is that an offence?"

"She's a very public-spirited young lady. She telephoned us and said that you seemed to know more about the murder than you should.

Despair settled upon me; my thoughts coalesced once more into headlines: MAN FROM MIRROR QUESTIONED IN BOURNEMOUTH MURDER HUNT. I doubted if I'd even be able to get back my old job on the *Dartmouth Chronicle* and so I told him who I was.

"Got your Press card, sir?"

Only a few journalists were issued with Scotland Yard Press passes and I wasn't one of them.

"Better come along with us, sir," the officer said so I climbed into the waiting police car and was driven to the station.

The nightmare was mercifully short when, at the police station, I was recognised by a detective inspector on the case. But when I returned to the hotel I found that the other reporters had telephoned a story about a mystery witness being questioned. If I didn't phone the same story then I would be interrogated by the news desk in the morning. I telephoned three paragraphs and waited while a night newsdesk man read my copy.

"Any idea who the mystery witness is, old boy?"

My lips trembling and a tic developed in one eye. "None at all."

"Pity, see if you can find out."

I nodded at the receiver clenched in my hand and replaced it.

All the papers carried the story about the mystery witness next day. But happily the evening papers said that he had been released.

And his identity was never divulged.

V

The flat which I occupied with my wife, Elizabeth, and our son Patrick, in Richmond was a dripping basement which was shared with cockroaches, wood-lice and a few snails. The garden was at eye-level and a toad used to stare moodily through the window.

The only advantage of the flat was its proximity to the glorious gardens that swept down to the Thames from the statue known as Bulging Bessie, the views of the river wandering serenely to its source, and good pubs such as the Roebuck and the Lass of Richmond Hill.

But the flat was no place for a small child so on July 3, 1954 — the day war-time food rationing was finally ended — we moved to 36, Baldry Gardens, Streatham Common, a modest apartment on the upper floor of a medium-sized house but baronial by comparison with our other seedy abodes.

We could play with Patrick, an ebullient toddler, on the worn grass of the common or walk him round the rose-gardens of the Rookery, a small sanctuary that embodied an illusory impression that the sea was nearby.

Streatham at that time was neither a suburb — suburbia began at Norbury — nor a Chelsea or Fulham, although it contained elements of both. Parade-ground rows of houses, Sainsbury's and British Home Stores incongruously blended with drinking clubs and blocks of flats that had about them an air of luxurious decadence.

In between Streatham and central London lay Brixton, not yet a ghetto, and Kennington and Lambeth, a hinterland of squat terrace houses shouldering each other towards the Thames. In the middle, a green island in dark waters, stood the Oval cricket ground.

Life at No. 36 was complicated by the fact that the tenants downstairs were also named Lambert. We shared a common front-door and a burgeoning hostility towards each other.

When I crept up the creaking stairs at 4.00 a.m. I would hear whining bed-springs and morose exchanges between the lower-floor Lamberts. Later in the morning when I was asleep the downstairs front-door would crash shut shaking flakes of whitewash into my half-open mouth.

From the front window Elizabeth would shout: "You've taken the door off its hinges Mr. Lambert," to which the downstairs tenant would reply: "Go and buy some new ones Mrs. Lambert."

These exchanges gave rise to the impression among neighbours and tradesmen that not only did Elizabeth and I live in an atmosphere of unremitting acrimony but that we only addressed each other by our surnames.

We chose Streatham for the usual journalistic reason: you could get home at any time of the night. We were on an all-night bus route; other newspapermen preferred all-night train services most of which, in South London, operated on a loop joined at the neck by Waterloo Station. This meant that, if a reporter slumped wearily into a compartment after a few snorts at the Press Club, he could sleep peacefully safe in the knowledge that if he passed his station he would be transported back to Waterloo to begin the journey all over again. Some journalists circled the suburbs two or three times before awakening at Putney unaware that they had travelled sixty miles to get there.

One or two reckless scribes lived thirty or forty miles outside London at towns where express trains stopped before speeding towards provincial outposts of the British Isles. If they overslept they were dumped at dawn at Plymouth or Cardiff with the milk and the mail, faced with the daunting task of explaining to Ken Hord on the phone why they would be five hours late for their 10.00 a.m. shift.

On the all-night buses to Streatham we were a wildly assorted bunch. Printers and Pressmen, bouncers, dancers, whores, musicians . . . joined in exhausted conviviality, like revellers supping the last brown ale after a charabanc trip to Southend.

I waited for the bus beside the Embankment Gardens at an all-night coffee stall that dispensed sausage rolls and meat pies that hissed with steam when you bit into them. In front of the stall the Thames slid past, sometimes shining with silver coins of moonlight, sometimes bedridden beneath a blanket of mist. Behind the stall, tramps wrapped in newspapers snored on the park benches.

Big Ben boomed; ships called plaintively to the distant sea. Then the red double-decker arrived already three-quarters full of night people.

"Hallo Bill, did you blow well tonight, mate?" a printer would say to a white-faced musician in a natty, double-breasted suit.

"Not too bad, tosh. Got a paper?"

And across the seats went a copy of tomorrow's paper stamped on the front-page in purple ink VOUCHER. First copy, of course, to the conductor who sometimes forgot to ask for the fare.

"Evening Doris, how many did you have away tonight?"

"Too many luv. All short-times. I'm bleeding exhausted. Got a paper?"

And off we went across Blackfriars Bridge to the darkened shores where the day people who had never experienced the cameraderie of their nocturnal cousins still slumbered. We felt a little sorry for them: they wasted the summer days at work while we fished or swam or painted the shed: they relaxed bloated after dinner waiting for bed while, inflated with fresh-air, we swung into our routine. The working day belonged to everybody, the night was ours.

53

Our leader, protector and entertainer was the conductor. He should have worn a red Butlin's blazer instead of shiny blue serge. Like their passengers the conductors were owls who only worked in the darkness, knowing each stop by the blue light of a police station, the silhouette of a church, the rattle of a milk depot.

They knew their regulars and if they nodded off they woke them before their stops. They were usually middle-aged to elderly and they regaled us with Cockney wit or jokes plucked and pickled from ITMA. At dawn they wilted, wearily checking their tickets and recording the figures with stubs of pencil held with fingers polished by the coins in their satchels.

Sometimes a policeman would swing onto the running board to speed up his beat; sometimes the bus would stop while the driver exchanged pleasantries with a mate bound in the opposite direction.

Not all the passengers were regulars. Shame-faced men with empty wallets, for instance, on their way home after a night in the wicked West End sometimes joined us. And we had our occasionals who boarded the bus once or twice a week.

Among these were two six-footers with dockers' shoulders, fists like hams and faces pocked with scars. One was white, one was black. Sometimes there would be traces of blood on their fists or strips of sticky plaster on their faces. Even if the bus was full they never had to stand. They rarely spoke and they left the bus somewhere between Brixton and Streatham.

One night before they left us the black bruiser stopped in front of a burly printer sitting beside me and handed him a scrap of lined paper torn from a notebook and disappeared into the night. The regulars gazed at the printer curiously as he read the message aloud.

It said simply and disconcertingly I LOVE YOU.

* * *

Back in Streatham on summer mornings the common would

54

be pearled with dew as dawn extinguished night and there would be a smell of baking bread on the air and in the hawthorn trees the blackbirds would be rehearsing for the day.

If it was Saturday I had about two hours expectation of sleep because, like many impecunious daily reporters, I worked as a casual on the *Sunday Pictorial*, subsequently re-named the *Sunday Mirror*, and had to report for work at 10.00 a.m.

The *Pic* was a very different organisation from the *Mirror*. It was run by a team of brilliant bandits, notably Fred Redman, the news editor, voluble, hearty and shrewd. The star of his reporting team was an unlikely-looking candidate named Harry Proctor. He was slightly built and shabbily dressed, but he had only to thump on a front door and all the cupboards swung open revealing the skeletons inside.

On Saturdays they operated from the *Mirror* newsroom but the atmosphere was profoundly different. What they feared most was a big story breaking because Sunday newspapers planned and perpetrated their escapades during the week and if a gunman went berserk on a Saturday they might have to consider removing their exposure of a debauched vicar from the front page.

If you telephoned the *Pic* newsdesk to report that there was nothing in a Saturday story there was a sigh of relief on the other end of the line. You would be instructed to go and have a beer "and ring in on the way back", the compulsive cry of every desk man.

The *Pic* was relentless in its pursuit of depraved clergymen and scout masters. And those who condemn this brand of journalism should pause to consider their reactions if their son, choirboy or scout, has been corrupted by some satyr camouflaged by surplice or Baden-Powell hat.

The reporters also brought to justice rogues with infallible systems of beating the bookies, con-men who parted lonely widows from their savings, schoolmasters with as many qualifications as a road-sweeper, slum landlords, loan sharks . . . one of these was projected every Sunday under the headline RAT OF THE WEEK. But the classic front-page headline, addressed to an iniquitous clergyman, was to the effect GO UNFROCK YOURSELF.

The principle opposition was the *News of the World* which so many claimed they read for the sports news — indoor sports presumably — and the *People*. Then, as now, the *Sunday Express* was the phenomenon of Fleet Street, declining to compete with such rivals but maintaining a massive circulation with clean, crisp reporting, Giles' cartoons and John Gordon's column which could knock a pompous politician off the Front or Back Bench with one slug of type.

The *Pic's* competitive forays were mostly in the buy-up market, often during a sensational court case when, with a flutter of the pages of a cheque book, a protagonist would be persuaded to "tell all" at the end of the trial.

Alas, the *Mirror* casuals and the *Pictorial* staffers never really hit it off. We regarded the Saturday stint as a chore to earn an extra fiver; they regarded us as stop-gaps and sensed our resentment. Aware that they were not our true masters we retired for inordinately long periods to Barney Finnegans to arrogantly await a summons from the desk. Finally I received just such a summons and was informed that my services were no longer required.

Not only was this humiliating it was for me financially disastrous because I had been putting away the fiver to save the down-payment on a house. Depression settled heavily upon me, a mood that was not lightened by my assignment the following day, the Remembrance Day ceremony at the Cenotaph.

Although it was a sombre day poppies bloomed brightly on dark lapels and medals jingled bravely. They died not in vain; perhaps not but they certainly died in mud and blood and futility. Old men marching proudly, still deaf or part-blind from gas or mortar . . . boys with soap-bright faces holding grandfather's hand — "Did you ever kill anyone, grandpa?"

But the old men do not reply. They hear the whine of shells, the scutter of rats, the whispered messages of the dying. And no, there is no glory despite what the boys beside them read in the history books.

I walked into the park where the big leaves of the plane trees were stuck to the wet paths. Loneliness is always abroad in a park and the Sunday gloom enveloped me. If I had known that next day I would be on the point of being fired from the *Mirror* then the gloom would have darkened to despair; on the other hand, if I could possibly have glimpsed the circumstances of the impending debacle, then I might have thrown myself on the soggy grass hooting with maniacal mirth.

VI

In the provinces my downfall had usually been sport. On the *Mirror* it was animals.

As so often happens depression can be replaced by exhilaration. On this Monday morning I felt positively skittish. It so happened that one of Betty Tay's subjects, a beautiful boxer dog, was waiting for her in the tiny waiting room outside the doors leading into the newsroom.

Madness suddenly assailed me. I took the dog's lead and led him into the newsroom and stood directly behind Betty who was sitting at her desk.

Now to appreciate the ensuing scene that could only be equalled in a Whitehall farce the positioning of the principals must be appreciated.

There was Ken Hord at the news desk with his back to us; behind him Dot Watson's desk which happened to be vacant at the time; behind that Betty Tay's desk. If Ken Hord turned round he would see only Betty's torso and my body down to some point just above the crotch. The dog was invisible to him.

With the madness still upon me I whispered to Betty: "Put your hand behind you."

She did so and, with unerring accuracy, placed her fingers on the boxer's whiskered, slavering muzzle. At that moment events in the newsroom conspired against me because there was one of those rare lulls in the noise.

Betty let out an ear-splitting shriek and shouted: "It's all hot and hairy."

Ken Hord wheeled round and saw only Betty Tay, hand behind her, and the top half of me standing there with a foolish expression on my face. He reached his own conclusions and summoned me immediately to the waiting room with the obvious intention of ridding himself of the services of a pervert.

I followed him in still leading the dog and in despairing, staccatto sentences tried to explain that it was not what he thought that had been hot and hairy. From time to time the boxer licked my hand sympathetically.

Ken Hord turned away. Had I discerned the shadow of a smile on the face of this austere but always fair-minded man?

When he turned again his features were sculptured in stone. He had reached a decision. He lectured me sternly about frivolity but didn't sack me.

It was, after all, an animal story.

*   *   *

For a long time after that particular fiasco I was on late night shifts and, on my few day stints, dispatched to tedious magistrate court hearings.

The first sign of a softening in the desk's attitude to the vulgar prankster in their midst occurred when I read in a local paper about a hairdresser who wanted to perm servicemen's hair. The bounder actually believed that you didn't have to be cropped bald to be smart!

On a day-off I took myself to see the hairdresser, Anthony Manzi, who lived in Heath-road, Twickenham. He was a small, delicately-boned man with dark wavy hair and a preference for bow ties.

He told me that inspiration had come to him when, as an Army barber during the war, he had finished cutting a recruit's hair. A sergeant-major had surveyed his handiwork and remarked:

"Call yourself a bleeding barber? The poor bleeder's hat won't fit over his bleeding head."

59

Private Manzi had suggested to the sergeant major that the recruit should be issued with a larger hat and had promptly been put on a charge for insubordination.

Miraculously the commanding officer had dismissed the charge and Private Manzi had vowed that when he was demobbed he would try and educate the Services into the niceties of hair-styling.

In a drill hall in Teddington he demonstrated his arts on six sea cadets all the styles of the day craftily combined with short back and sides.

I wrote the story and it was used as a feature under my name. Once more I was on the ascent, although news desk appreciation was grudging because excursions into the feature pages were regarded with suspicion.

During my time on the *Mirror* we had some outstanding feature writers — Donald Zec, Keith Waterhouse, Tony Miles, later to become editor and then Chairman and Editorial Director of the group, Eric Wainwright, Pat Doncaster, Alan Fairclough who wrote fine, fighting editorials interspersed with book reviews, and the lovely, owlish Marjorie Proops who occasionally swept through the news room as though someone was tugging an invisible lead attached to her cigarette-holder.

The trouble was they were all *writers*. They inhabited distant quarters at the end of a corridor, they were rumoured to be temperamental and they could take up to a couple of hours to write a story. We hard newsmen had to be protected from the decadent influence of this Bloomsbury Group inside our portals!

But the news desk was on the whole gratified by my effort. One of their kind had proved that they were a match for the Bohemian stars. *Just don't do it too often, old man. Off with you to Dagenham, a gas main's just blown up.*

My ailing career which had fluctuated wildly since I was sacked from the *Dartmouth Chronicle* on my twenty-first birthday was given a further boost by the arrival of a pretty American TV actress named Vicki Carlson.

The slimming cult which was to transform so many comely girls into knife-hipped, pimple-titted scarecrows was just under way. It was therefore newsworthy when a girl who had read about Yorkshire pudding and pease pudding crossed the Atlantic to put *on* weight.

She weighed 7st. 13lbs and in one week she aimed to add another 10lbs. I picked her up at London Airport and we started off the day with a pint of milk and a currant bun. At 12.30 p.m. we stopped at a pub where she disposed of a pint of tepid bitter as though it were a dry Martini.

Then lunch — a slab of steak, a pyramid of potatoes and two dumplings that could have sunk the Queen Elizabeth.

By the end of the day Vicki's 35–22–35 figure weighed half a pound more than it had when she left New York. The story made the centre-page spread, after the front page the most hallowed space in the paper.

And for the rest of the week *Mirror* readers avidly followed our attempts to fatten up Vicki like a turkey for Christmas.

She was a sweet girl and understudied the American comedienne Martha Raye. Although how she managed this I couldn't imagine because Martha Raye's generously proportioned mouth was her fortune and Vicki's lips were petite.

By the end of the week she had put on a few pounds and she returned to New York happy that she couldn't do up the buttons on her skirt, sad that she was leaving because she had fallen in love with London and, having met a few of my more rumbustious colleagues, had discovered that Englishmen did not all behave like Hollywood butlers.

I bade farewell sadly because she had been good company, happy because she had helped me professionally to the giddy heights where I was actually to be sent on an overseas assignment.

*   *   *

Le Havre on a wet Sunday afternoon will never rate high in the annals of a globe-trotter; but for me it was recognition and high adventure — Sefton Delmer, Rene MacColl, Noel Barber beware.

The story concerned three English girls who, to the consternation of their parents, were sailing to New Zealand with three young men. The *Mirror* located the yacht at Le Havre and I was ordered to report to Croydon Airport with a photographer, Dixie Dean, and a two-man wire-room team to transmit pictures to London.

I had never been abroad but I had flown — in the Air Training Corps — an experience which had forever dampened any aeronautical aspirations.

Barrie Mullins, a curly-haired form-mate from Epsom College — where we had conspired together to avoid any form of sporting activity — was among the cadets. We were grounded for an hour owing to ground mist and just before it lifted Barrie unwisely drank a pint of cocoa.

Somewhere above Box Hill a bored and irritable pilot decided to throw the Dakota around a bit.

Barrie immediately began to eject cocoa with deadly accuracy. He reminded me of a Mexican bandit, minus moustache, firing an ancient machine-gun at an elusive enemy in a movie. Except that, whereas the bandit usually runs out of bullets, Barrie's supply of ammunition seemed to be inexhaustible.

His first fusilade caught the heads of the cadets sitting in front of him. He then gave me a short burst in the adjoining seat and, as I ducked, picked off a few sitting targets on the other side of the gangway.

For a few moments he reserved his ammunition while everyone took cover. Then, when they prematurely emerged, he let them have it again, head swivelling just like the rotating barrel of the bandit's gun. He ravaged our commanding officer's immaculate uniform before standing up unsteadily for the *coup de grace*. Hearing the moans from the *wounded* the pilot angrily thrust his head through the curtains screening the cockpit.

Summoning up his last reserves Barrie sprayed the pilot's contorted features and sent him reeling back out of sight. The curtains closed, Barrie sat down and a few minutes later the aircraft bounced to a shuddering halt on the runway.

After meeting Dixie Dean, a greying-haired Cockney comedian, I tried to imagine Croydon, soon to be abandoned, as it had been before the big jets flew us out of a more glamorous age of aviation.

There were the Imperial Airways airliners taking off to fly with measured grace to distant Khartoum and Nairobi; bi-planes and tri-planes bucketing about among racing clouds; swashbuckling figures in goggles and boots climbing from the cockpit. . . .

But the glamour was somehow tarnished by the memory of Barrie's malodorous exhibition in the Dakota. And the memory did nothing to fortify my own trepidation as the aircraft trundled past the airport buildings, minute by today's standards.

The *Mirror* chartered Rapides for their aerial work, small but distinctive bi-planes fitted with a trap-door through which photographers could take pictures.

As we crossed the wind-plucked English Channel, Dixie regaled me with stories of how photographers had fallen through the trap-door and been caught by their ankles as though rehearsing for some fancy stunt-work.

We landed on a metal strip just outside Le Havre. I was abroad, on the Continent! In the Customs shed I smelled Gaulloise and coffee, listened to the language spilling out around me. This was surely why I had become a newspaperman.

In the town, near the waterfront, we booked into a small hotel where the concièrge eyed the wire-room team's equipment with suspicion and, it later transpired, telephoned the police.

Before confronting the skipper of the yacht and his mixed crew we decided to have a drink at a bar — a dim place with a monosyllabic barman with larded hair reigning behind a counter pitted with cigarette burns.

We ordered four measures of Pernod firmly pronouncing

the final *d*. The barman regarded us enigmatically and spat into a receptacle at his feet.

"Bloody frogs," said Dixie who had travelled.

"Perno*d*s," we shouted. "One, two, three, four," on our fingers.

The barman took a fragment of comb from his pocket and tried to force it through his hair. If he had possessed a waxed moustache I might have forgiven him.

Then from some dark recess there materialised our saviour. Tall, blonde, shiny-lipped, tight-skirted. And we'd only been on foreign soil for half an hour! She crashed her handbag on the bar and spoke fiercely to the barman. Four glasses of Pernod tinkling with ice appeared on the bar. We added water and watched the yellow drinks turn milky.

"You are English?" she inquired with a seductive accent.

"*Oui*," we said.

"And for why are you 'ere?"

We explained.

"Ah, the English boat. I 'ave known 'ere well. You want to speak with 'ere?"

We nodded, entranced.

"Then you come with me."

She put on a leather coat and beret and we went into the street where a saline wind was gusting in from the sea. In the daylight she lost some of her mystery — and youth. On one side of her face was a livid scar. Her name, she informed us, was Claudette.

"I like the English," she said, "because they are gentlemen."

We inspected each other with some misgivings.

She certainly seemed to know her way about the waterfront and we were soon on board the yacht interviewing its occupants. The story went smoothly enough — one member of the crew had already quit and we persuaded another, a lovely girl named Beany Thompson, to depart — and it soon became incidental to the presence of Claudette.

Wherever we went she materialised, ordering our food and drink for us, crushing the spirit of recalcitrant cab drivers, guiding us back to our hotel when we had drunk too much Pernod.

On the final evening, by which time I had become quite fond of her, she took me aside in the little bar where we had first met.

"Derique," she said, "you and me must do somezing together."

I made a non-committal noise.

"I could make you much monies."

"Ah."

She bent low over the table and whispered conspiratorially. "You must leave these men."

"I'm afraid we work as a team," I muttered as though we were a gang of bank robbers.

"Leave them," she hissed.

"Forever?"

"We go to Paris."

"And live on what?"

She looked surprised. "On the monies I earn."

And it was only then, naive soul that I was, that I realised that Claudette's profession was the oldest in the world.

I imagined the telephone conversation with Ken Hord.

"Derek Lambert here."

"Hallo chum." He could install a dozen shades of meaning into that one word. "Where are you?"

"Paris."

"You're supposed to be in Le Havre."

"I know."

"What are you doing in Paris, chum?"

"Living on immoral earnings," as I hung up.

As I began to laugh Claudette said: "You laugh at me."

"Not at you." It was impossible to explain.

"You think I am too old. Too ugly," touching the scar.

I touched her cheek. "Nothing like that," I said. "You're beautiful. It's just that I have to go home. . . ."

She stood up, tears trickling down her cheeks, picked up her bag and disappeared into the night. According to the rules of gallantry I should have followed; according to the rules of commonsense it would have been madness.

Next day she was out at the airstrip. Magnificent and tragic. Dressed in black with the breeze teasing her blonde hair.

As the Rapide gathered speed along the metal strip she waved and I waved back. As we rose into the lonely sky she was still there, tiny handkerchief fluttering from her outstretched hand.

And whenever I drink a Pernod that is how I see her.

VII

My modest success in Le Havre moved the news desk to send me abroad again. This time a little further afield to the Swiss ski-ing resort of Klosters.

Any suspicion of romance concerning the twenty-year-old Duke of Kent was considered newsworthy and, as he was joining a ski-ing party containing several nubile girls, the possibilities were limitless.

In fact Royalty only had to sneeze to merit a few paragraphs and any hint of a Royal liaison — Princess Margaret's name was being wildly linked with Prince Bertil of Sweden following the demise of her romance with Peter Townsend — was slapped across as many columns as possible.

"Should make this time, old boy," said a news desk assistant as though any story I touched withered to a paragraph down among the truss advertisements.

This foreign assignment was in its way more daunting than my excursion to Le Havre because I had never flown on a scheduled airline and was quite capable of boarding a flight to Swaziland instead of Switzerland from the ramshackle collection of prefabricated huts that masqueraded as London Airport.

I managed to reach Zurich where I boarded a train for Klosters in the pleasant company of a member of a troupe of dancers who high-kicked their breath-taking legs in almost every TV spectacular.

 I arrived at dusk in the muffled little town. The snow was

thick on the ground and the air smelled of burning pine. Lights burned cosily and expensively in the shop windows.

I booked into a medium-priced hotel because I hadn't yet got used to spending lavishly even when it was someone else's money and, as the Duke wasn't due until the following day, spent the evening trudging around the bars gawping at *aprés-ski* parties.

My reactions were unreservedly childlike. But, war veterans apart, only the rich had travelled abroad and the news that someone was taking a holiday *on the Continent* was received with awe.

The Costa Brava was just beginning to open up and you could fly there for a week on some decrepit aircraft for £15 inclusive. Hoteliers were only just learning to brew tea "like mother makes it", Benidorm was still a fishing village and Italy was only mentioned by insufferable show-offs. Ski-ing was a dangerous pastime exclusively for the well-heeled.

I located the guest-house where the vanguard of the Duke's party was staying and made tentative but, on the whole unsuccessful attempts to ingratiate myself with them. They were the offspring of the affluent and aristocratic; I was patently neither. And whereas a reporter from the William Hickey column might have managed to acquire the correct clothing for the occasion I hadn't.

This became painfully apparent in the bright light of the morning. I had hired a pair of worn ski-boots so heavy that I walked like a robot. At the other extremity I wore a black woolly hat which had been partially devoured by moths. In between the two a grey Army surplus sweater and a pair of flannel trousers tucked into my socks. Fully dressed I resembled a cross between a commando and Coco the Clown.

After coffee and croissants and a pipe — part of my image at the time — I sallied forth into the crisp blue and white day to hire some skis because I was determined to stick close to the Duke, despite the fact that he was something of a virtuoso on the slopes and I could barely navigate the camber on the road.

At 4.30 that afternoon I went to the railway station with a

sleek Swiss free-lance photographer from Zurich. The young Duke arrived perched on a hard wooden seat in a third-class compartment. Looking rather less than pleased to see the photographer and myself, he climbed out of the train and kissed one of the advance guard, a pretty eighteen-year-old debutante named Jane Sheffield.

The kiss was recorded by the camera and, as we had plenty of time — it was Saturday — the film was freighted by train and plane to London.

That night the party besported themselves keenly observed by myself, the omnipresent, uncouth and unwanted shadow.

The Duke and Jane Sheffield danced cheek to cheek and later the party played a game called Torpedo during which Jane was thrown across the dance floor by four young bloods and caught by four others. In my story I reported the world-shattering news that she landed on the floor and broke a button off her blouse.

The whole report and pictures were printed on the Monday and, thanks to the *Mirror* make-up geniuses whose brilliance was acknowledged by all newspapermen, the flimsy content was projected with considerable panache.

THE KISS spanned photographs of the Duke and Jane Sheffield across the top of page seven. Below that the magical information: *From Derek Lambert, Klosters (Switzerland) Sunday*. Then the story flanked by a rear view of the Duke kissing Miss Sheffield.

On the Monday I determined to confront the Duke and question him about his intentions towards the delectable Miss Sheffield. I was aware that you didn't directly approach the Queen or the Duke of Edinburgh but was unsure whether it was permissible to approach a young man who was seventh in succession to the throne.

In company with some of his Society friends the Duke headed for the slopes. Behind, nonchalantly carrying a pair of skis that looked like floorboards ripped from a condemned house, came his shadow.

We ascended the slopes on a chair-lift. I was several seats

behind a bevy of eligible bachelors. In my lonely position I soon became aware that the atmosphere of the day was changing. The snow-capped peaks in the distance were merging with a grey sky, an iced wind was fanning the pine trees.

None of this was particularly alarming if you could ski your way to safety. . . . Then it began to snow. MIRROR MAN LOST IN BLIZZARD. But even that was optimistic: I wouldn't even merit a *Mirror Brief* if a fair-to-middling body was fished out of the Thames. And I certainly couldn't count on help from the Duke who had so far failed to acknowledge my presence.

Dismally, with one red ear protruding through a hole in my woolly hat like a flame, I sat in my seat watching the frozen ground unfold far below.

At the top of the slope the Duke and his friends dismounted and buckled on their skis. The snow was now pouring thickly from the sky.

Now or never.

Not trusting myself on skis, I trudged across the snow and approached the Duke. "Your Royal Highness. . . ."

The Duke looked at me as though I were the Abominable Snowman emerging from the pine forest and then addressed two words to me. The second was *off*.

Then he was gone, crouched over his skis, down the precipitous slope. His companions followed him and disappeared.

At that moment the chair-lift stopped. I looked around. I was alone. Not only was the snow falling thick and fast but dusk was settling. All feeling had left my exposed ear and the cold was nosing through the sweater. I buckled on the stage-prop skis and began my own descent.

I skied straight into the first available tree, then plunged into a convenient snow-drift. I fell a dozen or so times and, on one occasion, heard a resounding crack which I presumed to be a bone in my leg breaking; in fact it was my pipe in my trouser pocket.

I finally hit the road an hour later in total darkness, unbuckled my skis and achingly made my way to the hotel.

By Tuesday the Duke was dancing more with a beautiful Brazilian girl than he was with Jane Sheffield, a fact that was duly noted across five columns in the *Mirror*.

On the final day I was able to exact a petty revenge for my mountain-top humiliation. I reported that the daughter of the owner of the guest house had told the Duke's party that, unless they made less noise, they would have to leave.

*   *   *

Le Havre, Klosters and lastly, before I finally broke out of Europe, Dunkirk.

I was briefed to follow a couple believed to be illicitly exporting antiques to the Continent and thence to the U.S.A. where anything manufactured before the Battle of Britain was labelled *priceless*.

The *Daily Telegraph* was also following up the story and I crossed the Channel on the ferry with one of their reporters.

The *Telegraph* provides one of the finest and most comprehensive news services in the world but, because its content is presented decorously, readers tend to imagine that its staffmen are of a retiring nature.

In my experience nothing is farther from the truth.

Like all good newspapermen they first collected and dispatched their stories; then they caroused with the best of us; in fact some of them besported themselves even more energetically as though released from bondage after dictating column after column of detailed copy. Happily my companion on the ferry was one of this breed.

In Dunkirk we booked into a quiet hotel where surprisingly we were greeted affectionately by the family. Surprisingly because the English are not renowned for their reserve in Channel ports and the French get bored with such observations as: "Ugh, look at that froggie eating snails."

There was only one vacant room. It was twin-bedded and we deposited our luggage there and went to interview the antique dealers who were so co-operative that we began to suspect that there was nothing illegal about their activities.

We telephoned feeble stories, visited the beaches from which the beleagured British Army had miraculously been evacuated in World War II, then set out to investigate the entertainment offered by the town.

By midnight, astounded by our capacity to drink beer, Pernod and wine without getting drunk, we were sitting in a night-club singing: "There'll always be an England," and watching a strip show.

The management didn't appreciate our accompaniment and, grumpily, we left the club, clutching our francs in our hot little hands, and inspected a few more bars. When we arrived at the hotel at 2 a.m. it was in darkness. We pounded on the door, rattled the shutters and threw coins at the upstairs windows.

Finally the door opened.

A sleepy-eyed man in striped pyjamas gave us a key and we stumbled up the stairs and went to bed.

At 8 a.m. I awoke with a severe headache and a mouth like a sewer. I doused my face with water and took stock: the opposition was still asleep, mouth open. The room was clean and neat but there was something wrong. Finally it dawned upon me and I shook the recumbent form on the bed.

"Our luggage has gone," I told it. "It's been nicked. Passports, travellers' cheques, the whole bloody lot."

The figure moaned, spluttered and finally sat up. "Whassat?" it said.

"Our luggage has been stolen."

"Oh Christ!" Moaning pitifully he swung his legs out of bed. "Where is it?"

"How the hell should I know?"

"Oh Christ," he said again.

We struggled into our clothes and went downstairs to confront the receptionist. It was the man who had let us in at 2 a.m., now dressed in trousers and shirt-sleeves.

I addressed him sternly. "We have been robbed. Please call the police."

72

"*M'sieur?*"

I explained in the time-honoured way employed by Englishmen to explain matters to foreigners, elaborately enunciating every syllable and pounding the desk with my fist.

When I had finished he said in perfect English: "But you didn't have any luggage."

"Oh yes we did," said the man from the *Telegraph*. "When we arrived yesterday afternoon we most certainly had luggage."

The receptionist frowned. "But you didn't arrive yesterday afternoon. You arrived at two o'clock this morning as everyone in this hotel knows."

And it was only then that we realised that we had returned to the wrong hotel.

Our truculence evaporated. He handed us our bill and we paid it. We returned to the original hotel, picked up our unopened luggage and paid another baffled hotelier.

On the ferry returning to England we summarised our experiences. The story hadn't been used in either newspaper; we both had pulverising hangovers; we had paid two hotel bills instead of one. Perhaps, we decided as the English coastline loomed up through the mist, foreign assignments weren't all they were cracked up to be.

VIII

History was once again approaching a crucial period during the mid-fifties. Bitterness between the Kremlin and the West was unrelenting; the Suez crisis was looming; EOKA terrorists were daily bombing and shooting British soldiers and civilians; Sir Anthony Eden and President Eisenhower conferred about "the worsening Israel-Arab crisis"; Labour's Harold Wilson, M.P. wrote three articles exclusively for the *Mirror* about his interview with the Soviet leader Nikita Kruschev. At home the militant trade unionists were on the move — the dockers were awarded another 2s. a day — and Sydney Silverman had introduced a bill to abolish hanging. And in 1955 The Pill had been discovered, although it wasn't cleared for use until 1960.

Journalistically all such stories were dealt with on a higher plane than that occupied by the hard-news reporters. The foreign editor, Cecil King's son Michael, a burly, likeable man whose expensive suits seemed to have been trampled on before he donned them, dealt with the diplomatic crises abroad; Bill Greig and Victor Knight looked after politics; Len Jackson industrial affairs. Like crime reporters they all became chameleons, adopting the characteristics of their contacts.

Of all the specialists Ronnie Bedford, the science correspondent, was the virtuoso. His eyesight was chronic but he refused to regard this as a disability; through thick pebble spectacles he perused documents of daunting perplexity and produced stories exactly tailored to the *Mirror's* needs, i.e.

74

brief, lucid and succinct. He worked on the other side of the filing cabinets in agreeable proximity to the ravishing typists and could tell a joke as effectively as any stand-up comedian.

From time to time we general reporters briefly occupied the wings of the big-time stage. Particularly if a specialist couldn't stomach sitting through a speech by some particularly tedious orator.

Thus I came to know some of the more hackneyed ploys of the political speakers:

Let us not delude ourselves. . . . Total delusion lies just around the corner.

We will never concede. . . . Humiliating capitulation in the offing.

We are united. . . . the party is in utter disarray.

And I quote. . . . designed either (1) to distract attention from the speaker's own shortcomings by dredging up a colleague's brilliancy or (2) to draw attention to a trifling discrepancy in a rival's predictions in the hope that it will overshadow some gaping flaw in his own logic.

Mercifully our excursions into these platitudinous realms were rare and our fodder was the vagaries of the man-next-door — a far more fascinating member of the Human Race than any politician — and the exploits of Diana Dors, Lady Docker, East End gangsters, the TV panel on *What's my Line?* and visiting movie and pop-stars.

Many evenings were spent outside the stage-door of the London Palladium hoping that the hordes of hysterical girls would break through the police cordon and rip the arm off Frankie Lane's jacket or extract a hank of Johnny "Cry" Ray's hair. It was the decade in which teenagers were discovered and they made the most of it.

Most of the stars stayed at the Savoy where a slick PR organisation master-minded their Press conferences.

One of the most spectacular was given by John Wayne who brought with him a replica of a pistol which he fired to indicate a passage in his drawling address that we should record. If we hesitated, this towering star — one of the select few I met who lived up to expectations — would loose off another phantom bullet with an ear-shattering detonation.

Guests convinced that a shoot-out was in progress in the lobby cowered in their rooms. Finally an under-manager cautiously opened the door to see what sort of mayhem was in progress. The Duke aimed the pistol at him and the manager, unaware that it was a fake, withdrew hastily and the Press conference proceeded on its cacophonous way.

Another Western star, as tall as a tree, was persuaded by photographers to lie in a bath to emphasise his height. He was an amiable fellow and agreed. However his amiability faltered when someone turned on the shower and we, the baddies, fled down the corridor pursued by an immense and dripping goody.

Television stars of the B.B.C. were lionised out of all proportion to their abilities. Whatever they said or wore was reported in detail next day despite the fact that millions had watched them the previous evening. And it wasn't until the advent of commercial TV on September 22nd 1955, that their self-importance was dented.

What's My Line? was the worst offender. Almost every week Gilbert Harding, an irascible intellectual, insulted one of the participants — the proprietor of a flea circus or a potato-crisp slicer — while Lady Isobel Barnett or Barbara Kelly remonstrated with him.

It was then up to a reporter to get a quote from the tedious inquisitor. The only question I ever felt like asking was: "Why take part in a programme that so obviously offends your sensibilities?"

Barbara Kelly was one of the brightest performers and on one occasion it was I who had to interrogate her. It was a lamentable performance on my part.

The deputy news editor, Cliff Pearson, had got hold of a publicity still of Barbara who had been chosen to play Peter Pan in the annual Christmas production in the West End. He handed me the photograph and asked me what I thought. I studied it intently but could find nothing untoward.

"What do you think about her knees?"

They looked all right to me.

"Not the best in the world are they?"

Not being a world authority on knees I shrugged and made some inconsequential reply.

"Go round and ask her what she thinks."

"What she thinks about what?"

"Whether she thinks her knees are suitable for Peter Pan."

Miserably I went round to the theatre where she was rehearsing and hung around the stage door clutching the photograph, hoping that Miss Kelly might have flown home on the end of her stage-prop wire.

When she finally emerged I approached her like a seedy private detective about to serve a summons, introduced myself and thrust the photograph in front of her.

"What do you think?" I mumbled.

"Think about what?"

I contemplated hurling myself in front of a passing bus. "Your knees."

"What about my knees?" beginning to frown ominously.

"Do you think they're quite the thing?"

Obviously assuming I was on parole from Broadmoor she turned on her heel and disappeared into the dusk.

Another Show Biz chore that fell the way of the hard newsmen was *Cinerama* at the London Casino. This was a movie projected onto screens that partially encircled the audience giving the impression that you were actually participating in the action — careering down the Cresta Run on a bob-sleigh or taking cover from a hurricane. It was immensely popular, due in part to a publicity-conscious management. Whenever Royalty or some celebrity arrived the newspapers were informed.

If Princess Margaret attended with an eligible escort photographers would assemble outside the theatre while earwigging scribes breathed down her neck in seats that just happened to be vacant.

On one occasion a peer of the realm whose marriage was rumoured to be disintegrating arrived at the cinema accompanied by a lady. There was one insurmountable snag to the story: the lady looked remarkably like his wife. The knowledgeable said she wasn't, but there was a quiver of uncertainty in their voices.

When the couple emerged after the show the photographers' flashes exploded around them. They climbed into a waiting limousine and I and a couple of other reporters gave chase in a taxi.

About half a mile away the limousine stopped and the peer climbed out and addressed himself to us through the open window of the taxi.

We could do one of two things, he said tightly. Either leave him alone or continue the chase in which case he would drive straight to the nearest police station. We told the taxi driver to take us back to Fleet Street.

In the newsroom frantic scenes were in progress, especially on the picture desk where photographs of the peer's wife were being microscopically examined and compared with those taken outside the London Casino.

Finally, on the advice of the office lawyers, it was reluctantly decided that it would be foolhardy to publish the picture or the story. Only one newspaper did so, employing the evasive tactic of describing the woman as an unknown companion.

The paper was immediately sued and had to pay hefty damages. I never discovered the identity of the peer's companion but always wished I could have asked: "Who was that lady I saw you with last night?"

"That was no lady, that was my wife."

*   *   *

One Show Business assignment entrusted to me was unique: I

78

was told to watch Liberace every night for a week at the Finsbury Park Empire.

The pianist was at the time suing the *Daily Mirror* for a libel allegedly perpetrated by Cassandra. The case was uproarious, especially the exchanges between Gilbert Beyfus, Q.C., a wily and witty old bird, and the defendant, Bill Connor.

The public packed the gallery every day to see Liberace who wore, for him, relatively sober suiting. I covered the case writing an intro and adding those immortal words "Take in P.A." which meant that the sub-editors should use the Press Association version of the evidence as they were providing a verbatim account.

Before the case began the office lawyers had decided that a reporter should visit the Finsbury Park Empire every night to see if Liberace did or said anything to strengthen the *Daily Mirror's* defence. The logical choice was the reporter covering the court case.

So, with a brief respite between the adjournment of the High Court hearing and the opening of his evening show, I was never far from the extrovert star.

By the end of the week, as the curtain went up on grand piano and candelabra and a smiling Liberace appeared in a glittering outfit, I was becoming distinctly neurotic. Sitting in the stalls I began to recite his patter in a low monotone.

When my neighbour enjoined me to "Belt up for God's sake" I merely murmured from my trance: "And now Debussy's *Claire de lune.*"

Liberace won the case and the *Mirror* had to fork out substantial damages and costs. A small outlay, it was claimed, for the world-wide publicity the paper had received.

I retired stunned for a long weekend in Brighton. But I retained a great admiration for Liberace's professionalism and his humour for which the target more often than not was himself.

* * *

The *Mirror* was nothing if not innovative. Not only did it briefly have its own Weathercock but for a while it had two front pages.

This unlikely phenomenon occurred because thundering great editorials, inspired by Hugh Cudlipp, were being projected on the front page. This presented a problem if a world-shattering news story, patently front-page material, broke simultaneously. The *Mirror* overcame the dilemma by describing another page as the second front page.

Irked by the annual presentation to the Queen of the year's debutantes the *Mirror* decided to select debs outside the umbrella of wealth and privilege under which Society teenagers were nurtured.

A *Mirror* Deb of the Year was chosen and a glittering ball at which Errol Flynn was the star guest was held at a London hotel. Unfortunately debs' delights were in short supply and reporters were called upon to fill the breach.

We hired evening dress from Moss Bros. and squeaked around the ball-room in shiny dancing pumps while sweating organisers from the Publicity Department urged us to ask partnerless debs to take the floor. I waited for a slow waltz and then, emboldened by a couple of light ales, asked a sweet creature leaning listlessly against a pillar to dance.

But the fates had once again conspired against me. After she had confided, to my intense alarm, that she was hoping to become a professional dancer the orchestra suddenly launched itself into an old fashioned waltz.

The girl floated like gossamer while I clumped around in circles like a guardsman executing about-turns in perpetual motion at the same time muttering "One two, three; one two, three" to which the only response was the squeaking of my shoes.

As we passed a group of executives my shirt-front broke loose and my black tie began to edge in the direction of my armpit. I heard one executive say loudly to another: "Young Lambert's drunk again."

When I finally returned the girl to her pillar, I bowed, smiled with trembling lips and murmured: "I'm afraid I'm not much of a dancer."

Although the girl was a *Mirror* deb she had not had the advantage of her blue-blooded namesakes' training in protocol and etiquette. "Christ," she said fanning herself furiously, "you can say that again."

IX

As the fifties slid by I began more and more to lead two separate lives. Professional and domestic.

Most men go to work, of course; but rarely is their immersion in their calling as complete as it is with a newspaperman. On occasions we reported for duty at 10 a.m. and didn't return home for several weeks; even a single-day stint could last fourteen hours or so.

The result was that with many reporters their work became far more important to them than their home life; Fleet Street with its nervous energies, flamboyant characters and snug taverns, more tenable than their home-ground suburb.

Many marriages foundered but Ken Hord, ever aware of this threat to the marital harmony of his flock, always tried to ensure that his reporters spent as much time as possible at home. I, too, *tried*.

By this time I had, with the help of a loan from my father, accumulated just about enough money to put down a deposit on a small house.

It was only half finished, one of an estate of terraces at Mitcham with front doors of many colours, postage-stamp gardens and car-ports. When we first saw it the wind was gusting rain down the street, a wheelbarrow was becalmed in the mud and workmen were drinking tea in what they claimed would one day be an open-plan lounge.

Several months later we moved into what was now a neat, bright end-terrace home at 16, Priestley Road. Ken Barrington, the Surrey and England cricketer later bought one opposite us. Turf had been laid along the fenceless front gardens, our door was a shining powder blue, black Marley tiles gleamed in the open-plan lounge.

At the age of twenty-five I was a house-owner; in debt to the Abbey National — the house cost £2,500 — and to the purveyors of cooker, fridge, red brocade sofa and easy chairs, furniture and a bright purple carpet which we must have chosen wearing sun-glasses.

Behind the estate was the rust-smelling railway line to London and a fireworks factory, part of which blew up while we were there. Tooting and Mitcham football ground was adjacent; beyond that Pascall's sweet factory which exhaled its pear-drop breath across the estate.

The centre of Mitcham, a tough old suburb where gypsies once camped, was run-of-the-mill with chain stores, two cinemas and some cavernous pubs, but one extremity was abruptly rural — as though you had stepped from one film set into another.

The heartland of this rustic retreat was the cricket ground, one of the oldest in the country. A green triangle surrounded by roads graced with tall trees. Mitcham and Surrey Second XI played there and sometimes, during the week, women's cricket teams which fetched the old men out of the library reading room. Incoming batsmen had to hold up the traffic and cross the road to reach the wicket, and on the corner stood a mellow old pub with a copper bar and an Irish barman where suspect LBW decisions were debated until closing time.

On winter Saturday afternoons I took Patrick to Tooting and Mitcham football ground where I watched the football and he got lost among the legs on the crumbling terraces. I became fiercely partisan vilifying the ref and the visiting Isthmian League visitors, bawling encouragement to Paddy Hasty, the Irish international centre-forward who "just nodded them in", Bennett the cool and chunky centre-half and, later, Alec Stepney the goal-keeper who was to find fame with Manchester United.

It was a scruffy ground but our own. In rain and snow, with

the smell of mud and churned-up grass in our nostrils, we discharged the week's frustrations. Before the game, on gramophone records as scratched as a kitten's favourite chair-leg, Donald Peers encouraged us over the loud-speakers to powder our faces with sunshine; at half-time seagulls from a storm-tossed coast paddled around the pitch; when the final whistle blew we surged triumphantly homewards or mourned: "At least we didn't play dirty."

Home for us was just across the road. Tea and hot-buttered toast and Richard Greene as Robin Hood on the unpaid-for television standing on the purple carpet.

Winter days in Mitcham were paradoxically brighter than those of summer when the streets were somnulent and the flower-beds patches of dusty defiance. The first snow was whiter than it was in the country; tiled rooftops glistened after rain; each lighted window was a lantern of modest attainment.

On November 5th our tiny back garden exploded with witches' brew, bangers and hornets' nests, Catherine wheels that refused to wheel, rockets that remained embedded in the mud, crackers that chased us round the summer-worn turf. On either side of us flares and Roman candles lit the polished faces of the neighbours' children. Afterwards we ate potatoes in their jackets, half-cooked in the bonfire that had devoured itself within minutes.

Just before Christmas we took the Green Line coach to Box Hill and gathered holly and ivy on the frost-rimmed slopes. Bought a Christmas tree for 7s. 6d. and draped it with tinfoil icicles, cotton-wool snow-flakes, glass baubles as light as spun sugar. Hung the lounge with paper lanterns and daily counted the cards on a piece of trellis pinned to the wall.

On Christmas morning, standing ankle-deep in toys, we drank a glass of sherry during an interlude between the annual hostilities between Elizabeth and the turkey. Then the recovery through the afternoon, a festive cigar, cold ham and turkey . . . and all around us, behind the bright-painted doors, in houses as compact as boxes of crackers, festivities taking place

equal in their diminutive fashion to any banquet at Sandring-
ham.

*   *   *

Once a year Ken Hord manfully tried to entice reporters'
wives into the esoteric world their husbands inhabited, to the
cricket match between the *Daily Mirror* and the *Daily Express*.
We were not ordered to attend, nor was it ever stated that the
presence of spouses and children was obligatory; but the
impression was subtly communicated that we should con-
form.

One by-product of this public-relations operation was a
growing suspicion among wives that we were a bunch of
pathological liars. How else could we explain Ken Hord? We
had given them the impression that he was the re-incarnation
of a Spanish inquisitor and yet there he was as affable and
avuncular as Wilfred Pickles.

Being a dedicated spectator — born with athletic aspirations
but denied the physical attributes to implement them — I
watched the first few matches from the sidelines. As I watched
most sports — Jim Laker taking all ten wickets for England in
one Australian innings, Manchester United winning the
League and Manchester City the Cup, Henry Cooper stopping Brian London in 2 minutes and 35 seconds, Lew Hoad
and Ken Rosewall storming Wimbledon. . . . It was perhaps
this unfulfilled love of sport that finally precipitated me into
the *Mirror* v. *Express* encounter. I suppose I had talked a lot
about cricket and, perhaps because I was tall and had acquired a
tan from a week's holiday in Torquay, I was picked to play.

The implications were terrifying. The match was billed as a
friendly encounter but nothing was farther from the truth.
Any reporter based in the provinces who was rumoured to
have any ability with bat or ball appeared magically in London. And I suspected that a war correspondent would have

been recalled from hostilities if word had reached our captain that he could make the ball swing either way.

Fervour was equally acute at the *Express* where later players included the Australian Test player Keith Miller who, in addition to being a brilliant batsman and bowler, looked twice as handsome as Rock Hudson, poor chap. Miller, who wrote for the *Express*, always declined to bowl fast because, being a sportsman, he appreciated journalistic opposition and saw no future in decapitating his opponents.

Cliff Pearson, our deputy news editor, was our captain; Ken Hord was also a nifty participant. Peter Laker, a sports writer, related I believe to the legendary Jim Laker of Surrey, was one of the stars as was John Checkley, one of the *Mirror* men in the North Country who was later posted to Rome.

One way and another it was an intimidating occasion for a player such as myself who had once been selected as 12th man for Epsom College Fourth XI.

I possessed a pair of buckskin boots — bought at a sale and one size too small for my policeman's feet — that had turned an unsavoury shade of brown in the attic, and a pair of flannels that had split at the seat after some long-ago gymnastic endeavour at long stop.

As the day approached my moods alternated between misery and acute melancholia. I contemplated inventing an illness but that would hardly have been cricket; in any case I was patently enjoying robust good health.

On the morning of the match a light drizzle was falling. I peered at the clouds imploring them to burst asunder but by 11 a.m. patches of blue began to appear among them.

At 11.30 Anne Lloyd-Williams arrived in her little black car to pick me up and we set off for Bletchworth in Surrey, stopping on the way to buy a new pair of flannels because, although we were known as the Hairy-Arsed Mob, I had no wish to validate the description when I bent to retrieve the ball in the outfield. I also bought a box to protect the other side of the coin in case the spirit of Harold Larwood was abroad.

The ordeal began in a cosy pub adjoining the ground. By

and large the two teams kept themselves to themselves but I observed with awe the *Express's* legendary editor, Arthur Christiensen and the most revered news editor of his day, Morley Richards.

Over halves of bitter and salmon salad executives chatted with strained cordiality to the players' wives and attempted to forget that the previous day they had threatened to sack their opening batsmen for missing the point of a story.

In the changing room my gloom deepened as I listened to the chat which revealed unsuspected nuances of cricketing expertise — and discovered that my box had been fashioned for some sportsman with private parts as big as Bow Bells.

The *Express* batted first and Cliff Pearson, a heavily-built but agile sportsman, stationed me at a point in the field where only the wildest of mis-hit balls would reach me. He also informed me that I would be batting at number eleven.

It was a beautiful afternoon, the rustic scene like an old sporting print. Overcome by the drowsy atmosphere, the sound of leather on willow, I lapsed into a reverie.

"Derek it's yours!"

I blinked and looked wildly around. Everyone else seemed to be staring into the sky. And there, high above me but growing ever larger, was the ball.

I ran to my right. The ball seemed to waver and continued its descent to my left. I hurled myself in its path but, because I had forgotten to replace the studs in my boots, I slipped and fell.

Then the ball was on me.

On my chest.

In my hands.

And everyone was applauding.

With histrionic nonchalance I tossed the ball to another fielder and clapped as the batsman who had been well on his way to a half century returned to the pavilion.

The *Express* scored 120 or so and, over tomato sandwiches and tea, Ken Hord was moved to murmur to me: "Well done chum."

The *Mirror* wickets fell like autumn leaves. Our spectators were grimly stoic while the opposition became exuberantly festive as though the runs were circulation figures.

Behind the spectators, batsmen who had failed at the wicket morosely practised the strokes in the manner in which they should have played them. One of the reporters who had run out an executive — the omnipresent peril in these encounters — retired prematurely to the bar to reconsider his future.

The run deficit was hopeless but, half an hour before stumps were due to be drawn, the possibility of a draw began to loom. This filled me with foreboding because, although I naturally wanted the *Mirror* to win, I had begun to realise that, if I failed at the wicket, I would be in good company.

Another wicket fell. One more and I would be out there. I retired to the pavilion and put on my pads — and the outsize box because one of the *Express* bowlers was hurling the ball down as though expressing paranoic hatred for all Mankind. His face was, I thought, vaguely familiar.

At the wicket two batsmen were heroically defending. The possibility of a draw became more likely every minute. And the possibility that I wouldn't have to bat!

Then the fast bowler, who seemed to have been retiring to an adjoining field between each delivery, shortened his run and promptly had one of the batsmen leg before.

Five more balls to play and the game would be a draw.

Shivering with apprehension, I began the long walk to the crease.

"Good luck chum," said Ken Hord.

The spectators were quiet, the fielders tense as they crowded round me.

I took middle and leg, paused and glanced round the field looking for the gaps and hoping that I might be smitten with a seizure. It was then that I recognised the bowler: earlier that week I had beaten him on a story. The smile on his face was a snarl.

The first ball whistled past my face with lethal velocity into the wicket-keeper's gloves.

Four to go.

The *Express* captain conferred with the bowler. The fielders crowded closer.

I swung wildly at the next ball and it shot off my bat in the direction of mid-wicket. I began to run but the batsman at the other end who had no wish to face the demented bowler shouted: "Stay where you are."

As I retreated behind the crease I became aware of a constriction in my movements. Perhaps I had pulled or snapped some vital tendon. I explored my thigh with one gloved hand and discovered a lump: my elephantine box had slid down my leg.

The next ball hit the box inside my flannels with an ugly thud and flew through the slips.

"Come on," bawled the other batsman, seeing two leg-byes that would get him back to safety.

I began to run but the errant box so impeded my progress that I bounded along in slow-motion like a kangaroo with a wooden leg. By the time my colleague was turning for the second run I was only half way down the pitch on my first. No chance of the second.

Three balls to go and I was out of the firing line.

The other batsman prodded at the next ball, shouted: "Just the one" and began to run despite the fact that the ball was heading straight for a fielder.

In his excitement the fielder threw the ball at the wrong wicket and I lumbered home.

Two to go.

Not a sound from the spectators.

I played and missed, a euphemism for a shot that would have looked better if I had been wielding a baseball bat.

One to go.

I prayed and promised that I would attend church every Sunday if I survived.

The ball hit me where the box should have been and, as I fell moaning to the ground, the bowler flung his arms towards the heavens and appealed for LBW.

From my recumbent position on the turf I gazed imploringly at the umpire. He shook his head and removed the bails.

A draw.

I sprang to my feet and headed for the pavilion trying to conceal the box with my bat and the agonising pain in my crotch with a grim smile.

There was a ripple of applause. Ken Hord clumped me on the back.

For the rest of the evening I limped around the pub adopting the self-effacing attitude of the traditional British hero. I was bought several pints but the ultimate reward was yet to come: I was never again selected to play.

X

When I first arrived in Fleet Street no such body as the Press Council existed and the procedures adopted by pressmen to obtain stories were sometimes sharp, occasionally ruthless and often boisterous.

The culprit for excesses of zeal was the fanatical rivalry that existed among the popular papers and thereby the fate that awaited any reporter who allowed the opposition to get away with an exclusive.

In terms of circulation the *Express* was the *Mirror*'s principal rival but a more private feud existed with the *Daily Sketch* because it, too, was a tabloid and it was trying to lure readers from the *Mirror*'s magnetic grasp.

The *Sketch* worked assiduously at this task and ultimately failed; but while the fight was on it was invigorating and its quick-witted reporters were to be feared, in particular Peter Stewart, the chief reporter who later moved to the BBC.

The *Express's* traditional rival was the *Mail* — neither were tabloid in those days — and, heavies such as *The Times, Daily Telegraph* and *Manchester Guardian* apart, the other two in the field were the *Daily Herald* and the *News Chronicle*. For different reasons, they were also-rans.

The *Chronicle* was a delightful blend of wit, erudition and poetic expression but sadly it was an anachronism. Its essays would have been better appreciated by coffee house society, its direction was uncertain and its projection of news stories inclined to be timorous. Finally it was devoured by the snapping jaws of its rivals and its evening partner, the *Star*, also perished.

The *Daily Herald* failed because it was in the financial clutches of the trade unions and, despite Herculean editorial enterprise, it had as much chance of glittering in the journalistic firmament as *Pravda* or *Izvestia*. It was superceded by the *Sun* which later shrank to its present small but explosively successful size.

Although I enjoyed the antics of the game — the car chases, the buy-ups, the subterfuges — engendered by Fleet Street rivalries I began to realise that some sort of restraining influence was needed.

This was brought home to me when the *Daily Herald*, of all newspapers, suddenly decided to try and prove that it was the equal of its livelier rivals and descended mob-handed on a story.

The scene: one of the big London railway stations. Time: the evening rush-hour.

Cast: the middle-aged father of a young girl who had eloped with a young man and thirty or so reporters and photographers.

Extras: homeward-bound office workers.

Take One: father alights from a train from Glasgow.

Journalists with or without platform tickets surge through the barrier armed with cheque-books and cameras.

The father, a thin-faced Scot, angrily resists all financial blandishments and shakes his fist at the photographers as they jostle each other to take far-from-happy snaps.

As the flash-bulbs pop the gesticulating mob makes its way down the platform, through the barrier into the main concourse of the station.

Pan right to waiting taxis engaged by newsmen to whisk irate father away to confront daughter and companion.

An overhead shot of concourse to show astonished commuters gathered around what has now become an arena occupied by scuffling journalists.

Close-up shot of taxi. Father is pushed into back of cab by

triumphant reporter. Door opens on opposite side and father is hauled out by rival newspaperman.

Punch-up ensues between two reporters and tottering pile of luggage crashes to the ground.

Reporter named Derek Lambert approaches uncautiously and offers sympathy, warmly grasping father's hand.

Father furiously tries to withdraw hand but Lambert tenaciously holds on unaware that father has only one arm.

Father's false arm becomes momentarily detached from his body. Horrified, Lambert lets go and the arm snaps back into place.

Father, now thoroughly enraged, turns on reporter who has barely participated in the fracas but has the misfortune to be wearing a light-coloured gaberdine raincoat that makes him conspicuous.

Father lashes out with good arm and knocks out some of innocent reporter's teeth. Blood splashes down his raincoat.

Action is stilled.

Still retaining some dignity father makes his way to taxi and climbs in. Promptly joined by *Daily Sketch* reporter who had hired the cab in the first place.

Taxi moves away.

Fade-out.

*   *   *

Such cases fully justified the creation of the Press Council which finally came into existence despite opposition from Fleet Street reactionaries. But one of the strictures against the Press which led to its formation was not, I felt, quite so justifiable. And that was intrusion into private grief.

The bereaved often welcomed the opportunity to spill their grief and it could be argued that interviews began the therapy of recovery. Such considerations, however, never entered the minds of some of the self-appointed arbiters of Press behaviour, particularly those who were motivated by private fears of the processes of democracy.

Whenever I visited a stricken parent or a grieving widow I was welcomed into the home. Out came the scrap-books — a boy in knee-length shorts, a Serviceman grinning fiercely and self-consciously in his best uniform — and out poured the memories. By the time I reached the garden gate it was I who felt like weeping.

Certainly there was at that time a case for reform of the Press. But those who today seek to further curb its freedom should pause and consider the plight of people in those countries who have no champions in the Fourth Estate.

A shackled Press is the servant of the tyrant and Disgusted of Tunbridge Wells would do well to visit a Communist country and re-appraise his indignation.

*   *   *

On one occasion I was, I suspect, the cause of disruption in my own parents' home.

Reporters rarely had enough money for exotic holidays and, after a week in some five-star hotel in Beirut or Nairobi, they would comb the sea-fronts of Bournemouth or Bridlington in search of B and B for a guinea.

Elizabeth and I were more fortunate because my parents lived in Devon, having by this time moved from Paignton to Babbacombe where they had bought an old grey house picturesquely named Picklecombe.

It stood at the end of a terrace of what had once been fishermen's cottages. These had been enlarged and were now *imposing residences* with *commanding views of the sea*.

In front of the terrace rolled the lawns of Babbacombe Downs, printed with beds of heliotrope and petunias, and fertilised nightly by dogs unleashed by their Philistine owners. (I intend to seek the advice of Sean Treacy, the landlord of the Queen's Elm in Fulham, on this matter because, in a column in the *Sunday Times*, he proved himself to be a considerable authority on canine droppings.) Fairy lights were looped from the flowering trees and, beyond the lawns, cliffs fell away to the far-below beaches where the waves hissed and sighed on the shingle.

From an upstairs window we watched the holiday-makers sprawled on the grass taking the sun when on occasions it offered itself; the artistes making their way to the Concert Hall, among them an up-and-coming young comedian named Bruce Forsyth; the pleasure-boats skirting the red cliffs that nudged each other towards Teignmouth, Dawlish and Exmouth.

We took Patrick to the pub gardens of the Mason's Arms, the Roughwood and the Royal and viewed Torquay, still the dowager duchess of seaside resorts, from the top of an open-deck bus like servants touring the master's property on the annual outing. Once every holiday we took the ferry across the river to Dartmouth to revisit the territory where I had ingloriously begun my journalistic career.

One winter when we had returned to Mitcham, my parents decided to let the downstairs accommodation. It was taken by a glamorous blonde who proved to be an excellent tenant and friend.

Everyone in Babbacombe knew her identity. Everyone, that is, except my parents; although they were impressed by the verve with which she drove her small car.

All went well until my mother told her that I was coming down for a holiday and revealed that I was a reporter on the *Daily Mirror*.

The blonde departed the day before I arrived. It may have been a coincidence: equally it may have been that she had become tired of the attentions of the Press.

As indeed she might well have been because her name was Roberta Cowell, former pilot and racing driver, who achieved fame as one of the first subjects to undergo a sex-change operation.

XI

By 1955 I was, by my own adaptable standards, fairly well established on the *Mirror*. Nevertheless I handled assignments gingerly during the first six months of the year because the mood of the news was political and politics for me were alien territory.

On April 5th, Winston Churchill, now aged eighty, resigned as Prime Minister and his place was taken by his undisputed heir apparent, Anthony Eden. Ten days later Eden announced that a General Election would be held on May 26th. Which, as far as us hard-news reporters were concerned, meant an incursion into the scene normally reserved for the *Mirror*'s political pundits.

For the coverage of the election meetings Ken Hord chose his more stable reporters. Thus I was rarely called upon and thankfully continued gathering background material on Ruth Ellis, a beautiful divorcee who had shot dead her lover, a racing driver named David Blakeley. (She was subsequently hanged amid a storm of controversy.)

Once or twice, however, he was compelled by staffing problems to dispatch me into the suburbs to record the hollow vows of the candidates. As far as I was concerned these jobs were irksome chores enlived by two prospects — the possibility of rowdy heckling and the desperate race to get the copy over in time for the deadline for the edition for which the meeting had been ear-marked.

But it was always rewarding to observe the reaction of party stalwarts to the arrival of the Man from the *Mirror*. Undiluted joy if the candidate was Labour, barely suppressed horror if he was Tory.

(It is generally supposed by the public that journalists adhere to their paper's politics. In my experience nothing could be further from the truth. I've known fanatical Socialists on the *Express*, died-in-the-wool Tories on the *Mirror*.)

The meetings which I covered were as dreary as I expected them to be but testing for my suspect shorthand. The trick was to pluck a salient point from a speech and start to write the story, keeping one ear open for any further momentous utterances. Then, if the deadline was approaching, belt for the nearest telephone, machine-gun the story over to a copy-taker and sprint back in case the guest speaker was being pelted with bags of flour.

Brevity was, thank God, the soul of politics as far as the *Mirror* was concerned.

After a couple of moderately successful forays I was entrusted with a speech by Harold Macmillan, the Conservative minister who, until he had been shifted to Defence in 1954, had been responsible for fulfilling an earlier election pledge to build 300,000 houses a year.

To actually honour an election promise was a formidable accomplishment, so it was with an unusual sense of anticipation that I set out to hear the archetypal Tory luminary speak.

The Press were as usual planted along trestle tables at the foot of the stage. When the great man appeared he was greeted by a ritualistic ovation punctuated by a few boos from Labour interlopers.

I was seated beside a reporter from the *Daily Sketch*, also a tabloid but politically at the other end of the spectrum from the pugnaciously Socialist *Mirror*.

Warily I observed the reporter from the Press Association. On these occasions the threat was always P.A. with its lightning and comprehensive service. If you weren't nimble enough your own sub-editor would have the agency version of the speech in front of him while you were still trying to find a serviceable telephone.

This particular P.A. man looked forbidding. The pages of his notebook were filled with flowing shorthand outlines, his pencils were needle-pointed and, worse, he had a runner with him to whip his copy away to a phone while he continued to write his report.

A hush descended on the carbolic-smelling hall and the *Sketch* reporter and myself opened our notebooks, both blue in unconscious deference, perhaps, to the speaker. After a few introductory banalities, Macmillan began to speak.

He was brilliant and I was aware that I was in the presence of one of the last great statesmen of our age. But his brilliance was a pitfall just as perilous to the unwary reporter as boredom. So absorbed could you become with his rhetoric that you forgot to take a note of it.

Most of the time I lagged behind him, jerked into awareness of my responsibilities by the *Sketch* man who took a histrionic note, frequently underlining significant passages and scoring bold lines alongside great chunks of shorthand as though they contained declarations of war.

Both of us began to simultaneously write our stories in our notebooks. By the time Macmillan had finished we had almost wrapped it up. But the P.A. man's runner had already departed to phone the first few paragraphs. . . .

Our predicament was identical. What, our news editors would demand the following day, was the point of sending a staffman to a meeting when they were also-rans to an agency?

We grabbed the notebooks and fled from the hall, taking the precaution of asking a weekly newspaperman to record for us any outrageous heckling.

There were two telephone kiosks in the foyer. One was occupied by the P.A. runner dictating with gusto, the other was out of order.

We emerged into the dusk and gazed wildly about us. Not a kiosk to be seen, not a single pub where we might find respite.

"You go that way," I said, pointing to the right, "and I'll go this way," pointing to the left, political affiliations of our papers still to the fore.

The first 'phone box to the left had been vandalised; the second was occupied by a craggy-faced man who sounded as though he was placing bets on the dogs.

Finally I staggered into a pub looking as though I was on the run, ordered a pint and asked if I could use the phone. After some procrastinating witticisms about reporters from the landlord I was allowed to use the phone on the bar.

To a background of "Two pints of the same, Fred," and "Watch how you go, Bert," I got through to a copy-taker on the *Mirror* who seemed as impressed by the fact that he was going to record Macmillan's oratory as a judge listening to a plea of mitigation.

Watched curiously by the customers at the bar, I opened my notebook and said into the phone: "Oh my God!"

"What's that, old man?" plaintively on the other end of the phone.

Speechlessly I stared at copy written in neat, upright script. My writing had never been neat or upright since nursery school. What I had in front of me was the story written by the reporter from the *Sketch*.

"Are you still there, old boy?"

What had I written? My mind seized up; I began to gibber miserably into the receiver. The landlord gazed at me speculatively and said: "Are you all right, lad?"

"Never felt better." And, smiling brightly at the watchful faces around me, I began to dictate the *Sketch* man's story.

Outside the hall where the meeting was taking place I met the *Sketch* reporter. We exchanged notebooks.

"Well," he said, "did you?"

I nodded.

"Me too. Every bloody word of *your* stuff."

"Well," I said philosophically, "we'll just have to wait and see, won't we?"

The following day my story appeared word-for-word as written in the *Sketch*. As did his story in the *Mirror*.

Later that month the Tories romped home with a majority of fifty-nine to continue their dominance of the fifties. Should anyone be so misguided as to believe that such victories are influenced by biased Press reporting then perhaps they should re-read this cautionary tale!

*   *   *

Although I was rarely personally involved in political journalism the events that I covered naturally affected Parliamentary behaviour.

In April of the following year, for instance, the Soviet leaders Bulganin and Khrushchev — "B and K" — visited Britain on the cruiser *Ordjonikidze*.

While it was docked at Portsmouth a Russian look-out spotted a frogman near the vessel. Subsequently a legendary diver, Commander Lionel Crabb, was reported missing.

Had the Russians captured him? Had he had been engaged on some clandestine mission beneath the cruiser?

The questions have never been answered. But the incident did lead to a barrage of questions in the House of Commons and an apology was made to the Russians.

A long time later the remnants of a body were fished out of Chichester harbour and identified as Commander Crabb's remains. But the cause of death wasn't ascertained.

Wherever he went the bouncing, bald-headed Khrushchev created news. Most of us following in his trail warmed to him and I felt that he crystallised my views on political standards with one quote delivered when he returned to Moscow.

Along with Bulganin he had attended a dinner thrown by the Labour Party Executive. But it didn't turn out to be the chummy affair that he not unnaturally expected.

Khrushchev's speech was subjected to a barrage of heckling by George Brown — another character for whom the Press should inaugurate a Thanksgiving ceremony — and he was questioned by Hugh Gaitskell who, in December 1955, had taken over from Clement Atlee as Labour leader, about the fate of Socialists who had disappeared behind the Iron Curtain.

Khrushchev was later quoted as telling the British Ambassador in Moscow: "I'm going to vote Conservative."

* * *

Just as a *Mirror* reporter's contact with politics was peripheral, so were his dealings with trade union affairs.

These were handled by the specialists and the nearest a hard newsman got to them was door-stepping a meeting of shop stewards at Dagenham. Which is not to say that we didn't do a lot of door-stepping, after the election there was a six-week dock strike and a seventeen-day rail stoppage.

For me the intransigence of management and union chiefs, both of whom know that ultimately agreement would be reached, was put in its right perspective for all time by the lug-wormers of East Anglia.

The confrontation between the men who dig the worms and the tackle shops who sell them to anglers as bait was covered by a friend of mine who worked for the *Daily Mail*.

One of the 'phones littered around the reporters' desks rang and, after locating the right one — always a tricky manoeuvre — he picked up the receiver.

Said the voice on the phone: "East Anglian lug-wormers here."

"Ah." Accustomed to practical jokers, the reporter said nothing and waited.

Said the informant: "We're going on strike. The tackle shops won't give us enough money for our worms."

The reporter frowned at the receiver. The mental picture of teams of lug-wormers leaning on their spades defying the tackle-shop proprietors was stimulating but hardly likely to throw the TUC into disarray.

"We're meeting the tackle men tomorrow," confided the indignant lug-wormer.

"Hold on a minute," said the reporter. Newspapers were always on the lookout for light stories — the *Express* invariably ran one down the centre column on the front page — and this had all the makings if, that was, the news desk could see the funny side of it. They could.

The reporter, an ebullient and bespectacled North Countryman, returned to his desk and told the lug-wormer that he would attend the meeting.

Next morning he arrived at a hotel in Ipswich to find luggers and tacklers already facing each other across a table in a room set aside for this milestone in industrial relations.

In the best traditions of such disputes there was an immediate hold-up. Both sides wanted an independent chairman and there was none to be seen unless. . . .

A wise old lugger pointed at the *Mail* reporter with one brine-pickled finger and asked him if he would take the chair. Why not? He took his place at the head of the table and picked up the gavel.

The meeting droned on. No settlement appeared on the horizon. The luggers wanted that much more pence per bucket of worms than the tacklers were prepared to pay. Deadlock.

Suddenly the *Mailman*, of a thirsty disposition, cracked his gavel on the table, said: "I move that we adjourn to the bar for ten minutes," picked up his notebook and left the room followed obediently by luggers and tacklers.

In the bar a few pints were downed and, with each quaff, the atmosphere became less prickly.

Finally a tackle-shop owner drained his tankard, called for a round embracing all the lug-wormers and said: "Of course we'd settle for twopence a bucket."

"So would we," said the lug-wormers leader, and the conviviality continued as though there had never been any hostility.

Next day the *Mail* ran a story suggesting that this was the way all industrial disputes should be settled. A message which is even more pertinent today that it was twenty-five years ago.

XII

One of the perks of the job was meeting characters. They could, roughly speaking, be divided into two categories — genuine and phoney.

One of the genuine personalities of the period was Brendan Behan and it was he who gave me the opportunity to drink in a cardboard pub.

When Brendan, the wild Irish playwright, was in town all that a newspaper could do was to assign a reporter to keep by his side night and day: lose him for a few minutes and you might have lost a story.

It was about this period that Brendan had appeared drunk on television and acquired a vast new public impervious to his talents as a playright.

During licensing hours surveillance was comparatively easy. You merely followed him from pub to pub watching him pour draught Guinness down his throat while he hectored, recited, thundered, argued and threw the occasional ill-directed punch.

The trouble was that he visited a great many pubs, most of them in the theatrical district of the West End, and the pursuing reporter took a drink at most of them.

By the time the pubs closed after lunch Brendan would be roaring drunk and the reporter well advised not to converse with the newsdesk until he had consumed quantities of black coffee.

But how could he when Brendan was lurching towards the afternoon drinking clubs or the home of some Irish friend where more Guinness and Paddy whiskey would be in plentiful supply?

One afternoon, after Brendan had been supping in the Salisbury, a fine old theatrical pub twinkling with copper and mirrors — the nearest likeness you could hope to find to one of the few remaining classical Dublin boozers — he suddenly decided that he loved the British Press and invited us all back to a friend's apartment.

The love affair, however, was short-lived. Back at the apartment Brendan decided to take all his clothes off. Fully dressed he wasn't visually a commanding figure — a black eye here, a tooth missing there, argument written all over his face — but in vest and pants he was black pantomime.

There was a child present at the time and, as he began to ease his pants from the lower reaches of his drum-tight belly, I gently suggested that, as it was very cold in the flat, he should keep them on.

Brendan regarded me with deep distrust. Were they my underpants? Was it my flat? Were they my parts that would be shrivelling in the draught whistling under the door?

The child didn't seem particularly concerned about the impromptu strip but still my Puritanical mind rebelled.

Off came the underpants.

"Honestly, Brendan," I said, "I should pull 'em up if I were you. You know what happened to the brass monkey."

This mild piece of advice brought unexpected reaction from the playwright. He pulled off his vest, stood in front of me stark naked and bellowed: "Who do you think you are you fooking English bastard?" and took a wild swing at me with one podgy fist.

I ducked as the fist approached ponderously. Brendan spun round twice and collapsed in a heap of pale flesh in a corner of the room.

It seemed time to take my leave.

But it was on the evening shift one really had to keep tabs on the unpredictable Irishman. He had taken to visiting the Met-

104

ropolitan Theatre in Edgware Road, the famous old music hall where his brother Dominic was putting on a play.

From a seat in the stalls Brendan would loudly voice his opinion of the performances, a critical accompaniment which not unnaturally enraged his brother.

The setting of the play was an Irish pub and on the final night I and the rest of the exhausted reporters who had been on the Brendan trail were invited on stage for a few jars.

In most plays drinks purporting to be alcoholic are usually concoctions made from burned sugar or something equally innocuous. Not in a Behan play, Brendan or Dominic.

I discovered that when the actors had been quaffing stout that was exactly what they had been quaffing. So for a couple of hours Press and players were able to join each other in a glorious booze-up on stage. Which is how, thanks to Brendan Behan, I came to be drinking in a pub made of cardboard.

*   *   *

Sadly Brendan Behan, like Dylan Thomas, committed slow but rumbustious suicide.

One late afternoon following a Brendan stint when I had handed over to a colleague I was able to ponder at some length — full-length, in fact — upon the difference in temperament between the English and the Irish.

I had for several hours been trying to keep pace with Brendan as he tippled his way from pub to pub. I finally caught a bus back to Fleet Street vaguely hearing such comments as: "Shouldn't be allowed on public transport in that condition."

Alighting near Fetter Lane I decided that it would be in my best interests not to return immediately to the office: Ken Hord understood the rigours of such an assignment but I doubted whether he would welcome the manifestations of them inside the office.

I decided that a brisk walk and perhaps a cup of tea would do the trick. So I began to weave my way down Fleet Street in the direction of Ludgate Circus beaming at friends and strangers.

At Ludgate Circus I went into Lyons, bought myself a cup of tea at the serve-yourself counter and prepared to descend the stairs to the restaurant below.

At the top of the stairs I dropped the cup of tea. Bending to retrieve cup and saucer I went into an impromptu and spectacular gymnastic routine.

I found that my head had suddenly become weighted and I was poised like a swimmer about to make a racing dive. Slowly and inexorably I leaned further forward into a perfect somersault. The impetus of this acrobatic feat brought me abruptly to my feet three-quarters way down the stairs. There I should have stayed hands raised high like a circus performer awaiting acclaim. But I was off balance. I stood poised for a fraction of a second before swaying slowly forward once more.

Ahead I was vaguely aware of a collection of women sitting at tables sipping cups of tea and eating cream cakes.

The second movement of the routine was not accomplished with the same style as the first because I had run out of stairs. Instead of completing the somersault and springing to my feet I crashed on my back and slid across the floor.

One or two women gave me a perfunctory glance, most of them went on chattering as though, every afternoon at this time, young men attempted a double-somersault down the stairs.

As I reassembled myself and limped towards the stairs one woman called out: "Here, luv, you dropped this," and handed me sixpence.

*   *   *

True characters such as Brendan Behan were rare and welcome to the Press. Less welcome were a few Show Biz personalities who worked at being outrageous characters; they were continually being convicted of drunken driving, and getting involved in night-club brawls particularly when photographers were present.

Someone had coined the phrase *Hell-raisers* and these insecure performers went to all sorts of ridiculous lengths to live up to the description.

The most tedious were those who played tough guys on the screen and decided that it was incumbent upon them to prove that their toughness was not confined to Thespian prowess. It didn't seem to occur to them that all-time toughies like James Cagney or Humphrey Bogart enjoyed pleasant social lives without having to punch guests through plate-glass windows.

The stories were usually leaked by the night-clubs where the fracas had occurred or, if the clubs didn't co-operate, by the actors. After one such tip-off concerning a star who, single-handed, routed bands of SS officers, Russian spies or bank robbers, I was sent round to his London home.

At first he indicated that he didn't want to talk about it but, when I prepared to leave, he began noisily sucking his lacerated knuckles and muttering that it would "probably be best to have it all out in the open."

He spoke as though it were an international incident rather than an unseemly scuffle at one of the in-nightclubs. According to his opponent, his knuckles had been grazed when his fist had thudded into a framed picture of the night-club proprietor.

The actor gave me a Scotch and told me how terrible it was to be famous. Wherever he went, it seemed, jealous males tried to assault his person. I listened with some interest because I had always been a movie addict and it was fascinating to be in the presence of a famous actor even if he was still acting.

Then, speaking as fan and not reporter, I made an elementary mistake. I said: "You're not nearly as tall as I thought you were."

It was as though I had accused him of having contracted an unspeakable disease.

"I'm five foot ten inches," he said. "Hardly a pygmy." I thought he was about to stand on a stool.

107

"I wasn't criticising, merely observing. I believe Alan Ladd is a tiny little fellow."

"I suppose you think you're tough because you're tall."

No statement could have been farther from the truth; for a moment I had horrifying vision of the night-club scene being re-enacted here in his home.

"Can you drink?" He demanded.

The interview seemed to be getting out of hand.

"Up to a point."

"I can drink most guys under the table."

It didn't seem to be much to boast about but I let it ride.

"How about going across the road for a few pints?"

I shrugged; it was obviously a challenge. I had no intention of ending up under the table but there didn't appear to be any harm in having a few sherbets with a hell-raiser; they might even slide the tankards along the bar to him.

He was greeted in the pub with a mixture of familiarity and wariness. "Two pints, George," the hell-raiser said and up came two foaming tankards.

I had never seen much point in swallowing a pint in one convulsion, nevertheless I had recently acquired the ability to pour a pint straight into my stomach without it touching the sides. Now seemed as good a time as any to demonstrate this virtuosity.

I put down my empty tankard while the hell-raiser was on his second swallow and said: "Same again?"

He gulped frenetically, came up gasping and said: "Of course," regarding me through narrowed eyes.

I took the next pint more slowly because it can't do your digestive system a lot of good filling it up like a petrol-tank at a petrol-station. When I moved I could hear the beer splashing about in my stomach.

He wiped the froth from his lips and sucked his grazed knuckles. "I like to drink," he said.

"I don't mind a few wets."

"I mean really drink."

"It's your round," I said. I was, I suppose, being as childish as he was; but he'd started it and I might never get another chance to swap drink for drink with a hell-raiser.

Three pints later he retired to the lavatory and returned looking pinched and white.

"Another pint?"

"Hell," he said, "let's get onto the hard stuff."

He ordered two large whiskies and knocked his back in one swallow in a creditable imitation of Burt Lancaster having one for the road before going out to gun down a score of cattle rustlers.

I took my time over mine while he ordered another for himself informing me that there was one in the pipeline for me.

He knocked his back, then sat down and fell instantly asleep.

The barman regarded him without surprise. "Always goes that way," he said. "Just leave him there, he'll wake up in an hour or so. Not bad for business really — like a waxworks exhibition."

"But doesn't he ever get fighting drunk?"

"Not here he doesn't. He only goes spare up West before he's had a drink. Mind you he never used to be like this before he took these tough-guy parts in the films."

"What was he like then?" I asked.

"He was as good as gold. Do you know what he drank?"

I shook my head.

"Ginger-beer shandy."

The figure in the chair whom I had last seen garotting sundry German guards around a prison camp began to snore.

*   *   *

Characters certainly had to be genuine to impress journalists because their own profession had a full larder of them.

Phonies were soon flushed out, even those doing passable imitations of characters. The exceptions were con-men: characters who created characters.

Some of them were so likeable — hence their success and the

leniency of their punishments — that you ended up feeling contempt for their victims.

The *mugs*, after all, were only conned because of their own greed. And in the late fifties and early sixties friendly English aristocrats were still selling Nelson's Column to American tourists.

Many of the con-men did the tour of Fleet Street offices where they were treated with wary respect. Sometimes they had watertight information to sell; sometimes they had already sold it elsewhere; sometimes their merchandise was as genuine as the three-card trick.

One in particular made regular appearances, a portly, balding gentleman who spoke without moving his lips and smoked fragments of cigarettes cupped in his hand. He had miraculously conned the authorities into believing that he was a social worker and visited prisoners in jail.

Instead of imparting messages of good hope he absorbed information about impending gaol-breaks and the whereabouts of hidden loot and acted as courier with such messages as: "Lenny says that if you touch his missus he'll have your balls when he gets out."

He also picked up a rich assortment of criminal gossip and it was this that he brought hot-foot to Fleet Street.

But was it exclusive? Because, of course, payments for an exclusive tip was much higher than payment for shared information. He always swore that he had brought it to us first because we were his favourite paper and it almost always transpired that he had given it to every other publication. Exclusively, of course. But there was little we could do about it: if we offered down-graded payment he would decline it with pained dignity and next day we would be the only paper without the story.

A good many unlikely looking clergy passed through our portals and not a few knights of the realm whose antecedents could not be traced in any reference book. Counts were on the wane but the occasional archduke still popped up from time to time.

110

One imposing, black-browed character with a news-reader's voice used to knight himself immediately he emerged from Brixton or Wormwood Scrubs. We called him Sir Fred.

Equipped with a nine-inch cigar which he never lit until he had clinched victory he then set about courting the ugliest and richest women he could find. They weren't in short supply and normally the only obstacle was Papa.

But as the ladies were of age — well over it in most cases — there was little Papa could do except employ a private detective.

This worried Sir Fred not one jot.

He knew his women and he knew that, in the class in which he was moving, the allure of an unscrupulous rogue was far greater than the appeal of just another name from Debrett.

He also knew that, when the denouement came, his current amour would set about trying to reform him and shower him with monetary gifts or presents that could be hocked.

If the stakes were really high Sir Fred, having tearfully promised to mend his ways, proposed marriage, a seemingly foolhardy course of action because he had been to the altar several times before.

But he suggested that the union should be legalised in some exotic hideaway away from everyone, in particular the bride's father. A man of the cloth was found — usually an acquaintance from the Scrubs — and a chapel that looked like a Gothic toilet from a disused railway station discovered in some remote Hebridean island.

Only when they had been pronounced man and wife and the champagne was flowing did Sir Fred finally light up his much-chewed cigar.

He was always caught eventually but no one seemed to mind very much, least of all the bride. She had about her a new air of fulfilment which might never had been hers if she hadn't met Sir Fred. Nor did she seem surprised at the other wives who crowded the public gallery to watch the genial bigamist get his due. After all she *knew* that he would return to her when he was released from prison.

111

The judges treated Sir Fred like a wanderer who had returned to the fold and, after the obligatory remarks about being "a silver-tongued rogue", treated him with surprising leniency.

If he had appeared before a woman judge they would probably have left the court together heading in the direction of Caxton Hall.

XIII

The most famous member of the *Mirror* staff was Jane.

She was the blonde bombshell who appeared daily in a strip cartoon and frequently stripped. She was beautifully drawn by a cartoonist named Hubbard and, during the war, had become the symbol of the girl every Serviceman wanted to return to.

Not only was she delectable with softly-waved hair and magnificent breasts, she was a nice girl. Thus she provided solace as well as titillation.

It was also possible to see her in the flesh because she toured the halls as a stage act. In our teens Barrie Mullins and I went to see her but, having obstinately refused to have my eyes tested, I saw only a pink and blonde blur, details of which were reluctantly communicated by Barrie who had fallen into a trance.

As a boy I had also studied the cartoon for any clues to the mystery of the female physique in the house-room at Epsom College. The *Mirror* was supplied daily; that and the provision of a snooker table were the only civilised facilities in that then barbarous establishment.

Garth was another famous cartoon character. He was the he-man to end all he-men and I often wondered what chemistry might have occurred if he had wandered into Jane's territory. He was also the catalyst of verbal exchanges endured by every *Mirror* reporter.

"Doris, bloke here says he's from the *Mirror*."

"What the hell does he want?"

"What do you want, mate?"

113

"It's about the allegation that you've called a strike because your tea-break isn't long enough."

"It's about the tea-break, Doris."

"Tell him to eff off then."

"Eff off mate and send Garth next time."

Other characters sharing the page of strips were Buck Ryan, Ruggles, the Flutters and an endearing little girl named Belinda.

By July, 1956, the *Mirror* could boast 11,220,000 readers, the highest readership on earth.

It was the common touch that did it and the regular features contained many well-tried ingredients in addition to the strip cartoons. Among them:

LIVE LETTERS. A symposium of correspondence conducted by the Old Codgers who daily displayed encyclopaedic knowledge and rough wit.

For Example:

I was surprised to read in Live Letters that only 7 per cent of the population is left-handed. When I once worked in a butcher's at Teignmouth, Devon, there were three of us and we were all left-handed. The cashier I took over from was also left-handed and so was the cashier who replaced me.

To which the Old Codgers replied:

Most of that 7 per cent must live around Teignmouth.

START RIGHT WITH THE STARS. An astrological column presented by John Naylor. Millions based their daily lives on the forecasts. Sometimes it was a relief if they were not wholly fulfilled. On Friday, July 27, 1956, for instance, I as a *Libra* should have "enjoyed a good day jam-making, bottling and stocking up home or business."

TODAY'S THOUGHT. Pearls of wisdom from the world's philosophers and wits. *Grammar is the grave of letters* — Elbert Hubbard. (The Hubbard I like best is: *Life is just one damn thing after another*.)

HAPPY GARDENING by Xenia Field. This column written by an enlightened lady who also carried out social work in prisons certainly had the common touch.

114

Who else could write a column about the Shoo Fly Plant and conclude:

Meanwhile, I have been asked for a Shoo Fly to keep the dog away, a Shoo Fly to keep the cat out of the garden and there was an urgent call from a lady for a Shoo Fly to keep her husband's girl friends off the premises.

MARY BROWN ADVISES. None of the stuff with which agony columns are filled today — sexually insatiable Cedric and microscopic detail about less savoury bodily functions. She purveyed down-to-earth common sense and doubtless there are many couples still together today because of her advice.

And then, of course, there was Noel Whitcomb, Cassandra, Donald Zec, Vicky's political cartoons, the fashion writers. . . . And Sooty!

XIV

I had by this time decided that by the time I was in my dotage, i.e. my forties, I would try my hand at writing novels. I was, after all, presented daily with the stuff of fiction.

One extraordinary story I covered seemed to be tailor-made for a future best-seller.

A housewife in the London suburb of Lewisham found a HELP ME note lying in her back garden. She took it to the police who rushed to the garden next door — and found a twenty-eight year-old girl lying on a rough bed in a dug-out ten feet under the ground.

The room was 10ft. by 8ft.; its entrance was a shaft of water pipes sealed with a man-hole cover; it was furnished with table, chairs, cooker and radio and the walls were covered with newspapers.

The young woman, an orphan, who had been missing for 105 days, claimed that she had been kept prisoner there for most of that time.

I was dispatched to Lewisham with a reporter named George Morton-Smith. George was one of God's gentlemen; he was in his sixties, carried himself like a guardsman, spoke with clipped precision, drank whisky with capacious but disciplined thirst and was frequently mistaken for the representative of *The Times*.

Neither the prisoner nor her alleged jailer showed any reluctance to be interviewed. I spoke to the young woman, George tackled the twenty-six year-old man.

The woman claimed that she had been abducted from her

116

lodgings at 3 a.m. and taken by motor-cycle to the garden-shed under which the dug-out had been constructed; there she had been kept prisoner although she had helped her *captor* to widen the room, working with a pick-axe and filling as many as eighty buckets a day with sand and clay.

Her *captor* had provided her with food and books and, on occasions, had taken her to the house at the other end of the garden to clean herself up.

When he left her in the shed while he carted away the dirt they had excavated she had pushed notes through the corrugated-iron wall, one of which had eventually been found.

There was, apparently, no question of her amiable companion paying court to her.

The man told George Morton-Smith that he was an inventor and he wanted someone to help him with his experiments. He had noticed the girl working in a grocer's shop and went to her house.

After "a good deal of persuasion" she agreed to go with him on his motor-cycle. "You cannot kidnap anyone on a motor-cycle."

He also made the comment: "Because we are both single we could not very well live together, so I gave her a room in the shed. . . . I did not keep her against her will except for the first few days."

All most illogical and mysterious and I don't think any other explanations were ever offered. But the story did make the front page and the middle-page spread MY LIFE IN A CAVE PRISON — *By the girl from S.E. 13.*

I duly put the story in storage for the day when I would write a novel based on the facts. Unfortunately John Fowles wrote a best-seller, *The Collector*, about a girl kept prisoner by a man, long before I left Fleet Street.

Did he, I wonder, find his inspiration in S.E.13?

*   *   *

117

If I were one day to write a best-seller, then I needed more overseas material. Something more edifying than chasing a Duke up a mountain or keeping company with a street walker in a Channel port.

When a big foreign story broke — a plane crash or an earthquake or a small war — I arrived early in the office and hung around trying by thought transference to make Ken Hord or Cliff Pearson suddenly realise that I was the ideal man for the job.

If the story broke in the afternoon I stayed late pacing around the editorial floor with the air of a man who would run the gauntlet of enemy fire to get his story out.

The news desk seemed totally impervious to my presence although once, while air tickets were being ordered, passports collected, photographers summoned, I was noticed.

"Derek."

I was instantly at the deskman's side quivering like a race-horse under starter's orders.

"Are you doing anything?"

"Nothing," I bellowed in his ear.

"We've sent the six o'clock man to Beirut. Would you mind doing the weather story?"

And so I continued to consort with gangsters, blonde bombshells and dumb animals. But I wished one animal, a magnificent gorilla named Guy, hadn't been quite so dumb.

The story broke in the afternoon at London Zoo. The gorilla had grabbed a small boy as he tried to feed sandwiches to him through a gap at the bottom of the protective glass between barrier and bars. I went by taxi with Tommy Lea who for some weeks had been assigned exclusively to the zoo.

I had always abhorred zoos believing that, by imprisoning animals born to wander jungle or plain, the custodians behaved in a more primitive fashion than their charges. But perhaps I was wrong: perhaps they were happy to sit in their cages believing that the human spectators were exhibits provided for their delectation.

It was easy to believe, viewing some of the *exhibits*: girls with high-sprung hair styles sagging in the drizzle, girls with orange hair rinses staining their necks, youths in stocking-tight trousers and duck's arse hair-cuts. . . .

The monkeys got the best of it eagerly pointing out to each other fresh manifestations of human behaviour: mothers searching for their young and giving them a good whack when they found them; fathers sucking spluttering pipes; everyone stuffing themselves with pork pies and crisps and emitting lemonade belches.

Guy stared at us and we stared at him.

What do you say to a gorilla who has just tried to eat a small boy?

Tommy took a photograph and Guy — so named because he arrived at the zoo on November 5th, 1947 — beat his chest with one fist. Which was all right for Tommy but how did I go about confirming the story? How had the seven-year-old boy escaped?

It wasn't the sort of publicity that the zoo authorities encouraged but, understandably, they were keen enough to acquit Guy and they parted with the name and address of the boy, Kenneth Keenan, who lived in London Road, Plaistow.

And duly Kenneth, with two stiches in his hand, sportingly told me: "I want you to know it was not Guy's fault."

Which presented me with a problem — writing the intro to the story. Something on the lines of *Boy forgives gorilla* was fair enough, but I had another angle.

Critics of the Press tend to exhibit symptoms of mental disorder at any suggestion that a story has been *angled*. Suggest that it has been *slanted* and they ran barking into the night.

In fact finding an angle is usually innocent enough: you have to discover some fact that will add piquancy to a story without detracting from its main source of impact.

But it can be dangerous. Intoxicated with the brilliance of the angle a reporter may concoct what is known as a drop-intro omitting to inform the reader that five men were killed in a gangland shoot-out until the sixth paragraph.

If the angle is exclusive then there is another lurking danger.

In the morning every other paper has the obvious lead to the story giving the impression that you have missed the whole point of it.

And this was my predicament. Before leaving the zoo I had been presented with my angle by a zoo keeper. But all the opposition papers would surely lead with boy-forgives-gorilla etcetera. In any case I wasn't at all sure that this wasn't better than my version.

The keeper had told me that the boy had, in fact, been saved by a chimpanzee named Abena who inhabited an adjoining cage. Abena and Guy hated the sight of each other and Abena had distracted the gorilla's attention with an ingenious ploy.

Abena . . . distant bells sounded. I telephoned the *Mirror* library and asked them if they had anything on the chimpanzee.

"Who old man?"

"Abena."

"Sabrina?"

"No Abena, a monkey."

"Oh Christ," said the librarian.

A few minutes later he returned to the phone and, sighing deeply, informed me that Abena was the mother of Benaudi, a baby chimp named and adopted by *Mirror* readers the previous year. Benaudi had subsequently died.

"He was known," said the librarian groaning as though he were biting on a bullet, "as Little Ben."

The decision had been made for me. Triumphantly I adjourned to a pub and wrote a story describing how Abena had saved a seven-year-old boy from being mauled by a twenty-two stone gorilla *by spitting on him*. The account was not strictly accurate.

The keeper had told me: "If you must know Abena pissed on Guy — from a great height."

*   *   *

The lives of such blonde bombshells as Marilyn Monroe,

Jayne Mansfield and Diana Dors seemed to have potential for a novel.

I only briefly met the first two, both doomed to die tragically. But in any case the general news reporter's favourite was Diana Dors. She was friendly, earthy and lazily sexy and what's more she was home-grown. She was a star and yet she was the girl next door. But not my next door. . . .

She drove an American convertible as long as a Thames barge and mixed with a colourful lot of personalities such as a ragged tough guy named Tommy Yeardye who was, I believe, a stand-in for Victor Mature, one of the then Hollywood heavies.

Instructions to find her after some of her more flamboyant exploits were always welcomed because she lived expansively and our expense accounts profited accordingly. One of her haunts was the Star in Belgravia, an in-pub run by an Irishman named Paddy Kennedy who possessed a brogue as thick as Liffy mud, a face battered by the storms of life and eyes as blue-bright as a Jager diamond. If you were merely *in* you drank downstairs; if you were really *in* you adjourned upstairs to consume large Scotches with Paddy; thus when composing your expenses you added a memorandum pointing out that you had been entertaining *upstairs* at Paddy's.

One day when the Fleet Street pack was hunting Tommy Yeardye to find out the whereabouts of a temporary missing Miss Dors I was sitting in the back of the office car in Mayfair composing my piece for the first edition.

As Mr. Yeardye was built like a brick store-house and, although tall, I was on the narrow side, I was somewhat surprised when a reporter from another paper approached the car, knelt on the pavement and asked me if I was the missing muscle-man.

It was dusk and I presumed I must have borne some shadowy resemblance to Mr. Yeardye. Madness suddenly assailed me and in a strange croaking voice I said: "Indeed I am. What can I do for you?"

A stream of questions followed which I answered in monosyllables interjecting the occasional "No comment" or "Don't quote me on that."

God knows why I embarked upon the deception. I dislike hoaxes at the best of times and this pathetic practical joke was getting sourer by the minute as the opposition scribe exultantly noted my comments.

Finally he touched his forelock, muttered: "Thank you, Mr. Yeardye" and belted towards the nearest telephone box. And it was only as I watched him feeding coins into the slot that the terrible truth dawned upon me: he had an exclusive interview and I had nothing.

I leaped from the car, ran to the kiosk and snatched the phone from his hand yelling: "It's me you bloody idiot!"

There was a long embarrassed silence while I reflected that it was I who was the bloody idiot. Then he replaced the receiver and walked silently away into the dusk.

We met many times after that but the incident was never again mentioned.

* * *

Gangsters were, of course, naturals to be filed away for future literary endeavour.

I attended the funeral of one luckless participant who had been on the wrong end of a gangland vendetta. The faces of the pall-bearers were seamed with razor scars as were those of most of the mourners.

The wreaths were so exotic that the possibility occurred to me that the outbreaks of violence were being incited by a consortium of unscrupulous florists.

My most unpleasant brush with the underworld occurred after a notorious hoodlum had been found not guilty on some charges of violence at the Old Bailey.

Other defendants were convicted and from the public gallery their wives booed and hissed and were forcibly ejected kicking and scratching and weeping loudly.

The gangsters' wives were usually magnificent creatures

with hair dyed blonde, black or red and wearing ankle-straps, tight skirts and fur stoles. They were fiercely loyal to their husbands and, if these gentlemen had been sent down for ten years or so, you could reasonably expect a punch in the mouth if you approached them. Equally if their husbands were found not guilty you could reasonably expect them to pose for the photographers on hubby's arm and utter that immortal quote: "Justice has been done."

Not in this case. I approached the wife of the acquitted defendant who, for reasons that I never ascertained, clouted me round the face with her handbag. She was then joined by three sobbing grass widows and her husband, a dark-suited figure with a face that had in its time contained as many stitches as his suit. He had apparently seen me approach his wife because he came dangerously close to me and suggested the physically impossible.

The quintet then climbed into a taxi and were driven away at speed.

Unfortunately I and the other assembled Pressmen knew the address of the acquitted man and we couldn't serve short shift by stating that he *last night declined to comment* — the journalistic euphemism for being told to eff off.

When we arrived at the block of flats in the East End where he lived we found the stairs to his top-floor apartment barred by two men built like Saturday afternoon wrestlers who also declined to be quoted. We adjourned to the nearest pub to plan our strategy. At first I whole-heartedly agreed that extreme caution amounting to total passivity should be the dominant theme.

Several whiskies later I embarked on a lunatic plan that must have had its origins in some silent version of Tarzan and the Apes that I had as a child seen at our local flea-pit. If I couldn't get any quotes, I reasoned in my liquor-fuddled mind, I could at least describe how the man in the top flat was celebrating his acquittal.

How? Simple enough, you mad brave fool. There was an open sky-light above the apartment. The block was separated from another identical block by a gap of a few feet. Ascend the stairs in the adjoining block, leap across the gap and peer through the sky-light.

When I reached the roof the view below seemed to be much the same as that from the top of the Eiffel Tower and the gap between the two buildings as wide as Cheddar Gorge.

The palms of my hands were greased with sweat, but the alcohol was racing in my veins. I jumped, landed on the other roof, stumbled and fell with my legs dangling through the sky-light.

There was a pause while I administered my own last rites. Then from the room below came a terrible voice: "Don't just hang around, come in."

I lowered myself into the room and embarked upon a series of ludicrous apologies to the shirt-sleeved terror of the underworld who was eating bread and cheese and drinking from a bottle of brown ale.

He seemed as stupefied as I was. "You mean you jumped?"

I nodded hoping that perhaps he thought I had fallen out of an aeroplane.

"Christ," he said.

A glimmer of hope. Perhaps instead of a gangland execution he would merely shoot off a knee-cap.

"Christ," he said again. "Were you pissed?"

I hung my head penitently.

He stood up and opened the door. "I tell you what," he said, "you've got guts. As you say you were pissed you can piss off."

The door closed behind me and I made my way down the stairs smirking horribly at the two guards.

When I was subsequently asked how I managed to obtain an exclusive description of the acquitted prisoner relaxing I said: "I just dropped in."

XV

The story that had every young Fleet Street reporter aspiring to be a foreign correspondent pawing the floors of newsrooms with nervous excitement broke in the autumn of 1956.

Earlier in the summer Gamal Abdul Nasser, the Egyptian leader, had arbitrarily nationalised the Suez Canal. Britain which had reluctantly withdrawn from the Canal Zone in 1954 reacted angrily; so did France which had built the Canal; so did Israel which was already under threat from Egypt.

In October Anthony Eden, a sick man, conferred with the French. The plan was for Israel to sweep into the attack across the Sinai Desert; Britain and France would then order both the Israelis and Egyptians to pull back from the Canal Zone and move in to protect it.

On October 29 Israel attacked across the Sinai. At the same time British and French troops were gathering for an assault on Port Said — and with them accredited newspapermen.

Throughout these preliminary moves I circled the news desk like a seagull waiting for food; leaned against pillars nonchalantly thumbing through my passport; let it be known in the pubs that my Arabic was immaculate.

Slowly hope withered into despair. Howard Johnson was dispatched, as was Peter Woods who somehow managed to convince the paratroopers that he was a seasoned parachutist.

Journalistically, Peter became the star of the show. Because it took considerable initiative and courage — especially if you were a 6 foot 5 inch heavyweight — to make your first and only drop into the muzzles of the Egyptian guns.

Meanwhile, back at the buildings, I continued to keep the British public informed about the weather and the life expectation of the inmates of the Battersea Dogs Home.

Until one morning when, as I was at home moodily drinking my tea and contemplating a new career as a cloakroom attendant or bookie's runner, the telephone rang.

It was Ken Hord. The *Mirror*, he said, had decided to extend its coverage of the Suez Crisis and dispatch a home-based reporter to Israel. Was I prepared to go? Did Sherlock Holmes smoke a pipe!

Had I had the necessary jabs? Of course; since arriving in Fleet Street my bum had been perforated with injections against every known disease that flourished in far-flung outposts in case the call came.

Was my wife prepared to let me go? "She understands," I said softly and dramatically.

And my passport. . . . There it was in my hot little hand stamped with visas, which I had obtained on my days off, for potential trouble spots from Harwich to Hong Kong.

"All right, chum. Good luck. Take care of yourself."

That evening I was on a plane bound for Tel Aviv.

The aircraft was packed with Israelis apprehensive about the outcome of the war and the fortunes of their soldiers advancing on the Suez Canal through the desert.

For entirely different reasons I was as apprehensive as the best of them. I had never been on a major foreign assignment; I had no idea what to do on arrival on Israeli soil; in fact I wasn't really sure how to send a cable.

Foreign correspondents are sometimes asked to name the most important qualification of their calling. To my mind there is only one answer: know your communications.

What is the point of a scoop if you can't transmit it to your paper?

Peter Younghusband of the *Daily Mail* (now with *Newsweek*), a reporter as physically enormous as Peter Woods, was a virtuoso in the communications game. Drop him in the bush five hundred miles from the nearest phone or carrier pigeon and you could be sure he would get his copy out.

Manuals on journalism should include a chapter on GET-TING THE STORY OUT. For instance, always send a series of short cables if they're urgent; cable office clerks who have to count every word have a habit of consigning verbose messages to the bottom of the pile.

And make sure that your office in London puts in fixed-time telephone calls to you; there might be a horrendous back-log of outgoing calls but that doesn't affect the incoming ones.

It goes without saying that one should always chat up girls on switchboards, although the consequences can be traumatic.

One of the finest communications operations in the annals of reporting was carried out by a *Daily Expressman* holed up in some beleagured city where rigid censorship had been imposed. The *Expressman* put in calls to all his paper's bureaux; to each he managed to dictate one sentence of copy before being cut off. Each bureau then transmitted their one sentence to London where a complete story was assembled.

Perhaps the most succinct cable of them all was dispatched by the Far East correspondent of one august journal. He was asked when he thought a particular military campaign would stop.

He replied: "Balls not made of crystal."

Weeks later he received a letter requesting him to moderate the language in his cables because office secretaries read them.

But the arts and pitfalls of sending foreign copy were as mysterious to me as nuclear physics as I winged my way across the darkened waters of the Mediterranean, bargain-basement portable typewriter between my knees, travellers' cheques, currency and authority to cable COLLECT in my wallet.

Half an hour out of Tel Aviv the lights inside the aircraft went out. I asked a stewardess why and she replied cheerfully that we were being attacked by Egyptian fighters.

Perhaps she possessed an over-developed imagination,

127

perhaps the Egyptian pilots couldn't find us; anyway the attack never materialised and an hour later I was standing alone in the main concourse of Tel Aviv airport thronged with purposeful Israelis.

You could feel the war, smell it. The exultation of Jews united by battle. Uniforms everywhere. Strapping soldiers weighted with guns.

For a moment I wished desperately that I was once again a mere *Daily Mirror Weathercock*, then I strode out into the sweating night, climbed into a taxi and told the driver to take me to the hotel favoured by foreign correspondents, the Dan.

I shared a room and bathroom, complete with sunken bath, with the *Daily Herald* man, Maurice Fagence, a seasoned campaigner and entertaining companion who took me under his wing.

He was a crumpled sort of man with sleek but dishevelled grey hair. From him I learned, as he took me through the blacked-out streets to the Press headquarters, that the fighting this side of the canal was virtually over. The Israelis had swept arrogantly through the Sinai and were now only concerned with mopping up operations.

The Press building was packed with dusty correspondents in desert-boots attacking their typewriters and cursing the censors. They had just returned from the Sinai; they had seen the war and they were reporting it.

What had I got to send to London? An incoherent conversation with a Hebrew-speaking taxi-driver, that's what. Instead, guided by Maurice, I cabled the rivetting information that I had arrived and was staying at the Dan. Then I sat back in despair to observe the professionals.

Famous correspondents from all over the world machine-gunning their typewriters and exchanging information about military tactics, armaments, political manoeuvring, referring to cabinet ministers and Army commanders by their first names.

They exuded authority and, equally alarming for the unblooded novice, seemed to be on intimate terms with each

128

other as though they were all members of a travelling troupe.

Among them I noticed Donald Wise, of the *Daily Express* who later moved to the *Mirror*. You couldn't really miss him because he was a rangy 6 foot 4 inches or so, equipped with a fierce moustache and a desert tan and looked like a pirate.

As was his habit Donald had been filing a stream of exclusives to the *Express*. Subsequently he and I became great mates, crossing many a "crocodile-infested river" together, but at the time I was the first-former gazing with awe at a swashbuckling head prefect.

I won't elaborate on his professional exploits because I can see him now in a bar in Hong Kong, where he now resides, incandescent with rage at my "preposterous impudence". Having witnessed him, as immaculately dressed as a Mississippi steamboat dude, toss a hulking bruiser across a bar with a twirl of one finger, I have no wish to provoke his wrath.

Miserably, I made my way back to the hotel with Maurice Fagence trying my best to absorb the atmosphere but hardly in a receptive state of mind.

At the bar Maurice bought me a beer and tried to revive my spirits by recalling his most disastrous experiences in times of war. He also came out with an explanation of the outbreak of World War II which historians have missed. According to Maurice, on his second beer, it was all down to a football reporter working for an agency.

"Absolutely true, old boy. He was reporting a game between Walsall and some other bloody team. He told a copytaker that riots had broken out at Walsall but the copytaker took it down as Warsaw. Hey presto, war!"

Next morning the situation brightened up a bit. I was invited with some other late-comers to travel across the Sinai in a bus with a detachment of soldiers.

It brightened up even more when I discovered that the soldiers were all girls. Beautiful, provocative and militant; a bus-load of curvaceous Mrs. Pankhursts.

For hours we rattled through the desert, bleak, brown and intimidating beneath a hot blue sky, stopping to view devas-

129

tated Egyptian tanks, heaps of abandoned arms and straggling lines of prisoners.

The girl sitting beside me was a talker, a fount of information about the undeniable achievements of her people who, although encircled by hostile neighbours, had dug themselves into the desert and made it blossom.

As she was a big girl, expert in the arts of Judo, so she told me, I listened with maximum interest, especially when she confided that she had been a member of the anti-British Stern gang.

"I hated you," she said. "Loathed you," in case I hadn't fully understood.

I made a non-committal reply.

"But no longer. We are brothers."

She embraced me heartily.

We stopped short of what remained of the front line and chatted with Israeli soldiers, tough and hard-muscled and exuberant with victory.

Then, leaving the girls with them, we returned to Tel Aviv to send our stories. I filed at inordinate length and learned later that my descriptive gems had been allotted two paragraphs in the general story. In the first place it was all old stuff; in the second the Suez Crisis was sharing the space with the Russian offensive in Budapest.

For me the war was over.

*   *   *

I lingered another few days in the vibrant city of Tel Aviv cabling a few morsels of copy, feeling the pulse of the place quicken with victory, waiting for my recall. . . .

Instead I was dispatched to Cyprus where a back-up was needed for the reporters in Port Said who had landed there with the Anglo-French forces on November 5th-6th. I also had to take over coverage of the Eoka terrorist campaign.

I caught a flight to Nicosia and booked into the Ledra Palace where by now Pressmen were looked upon as residents. It was a comfortable hotel with a vaguely Tyrolean bar where a thinning-haired barman made inroads into our expenses playing liar-dice, and a restaurant overlooking spring-like gardens which brought a little solace to hungover reporters and photographers at breakfast.

To stand any chance of survival you had to offer the hand of friendship to Savas, the night porter. He wore an immaculate blue uniform, his hair was oiled perfection and he talked with his hands as much as his lips.

Savas knew where a news story had broken and often, with foresight that we never questioned, where it was *about* to break. Before dining out we would ask Savas if he approved of our choice of restaurant. If he shook his head sadly then we gave it a wide berth because the chances were that you would receive a hand-grenade in the middle of your meat balls.

He ran copy to the cable office, appeased foreign editors on the telephone, whistled up cabs from a deserted courtyard and discovered a piece of grit in his eye when a nurse or air stewardess was being propelled up the staircase to the bedrooms.

When I arrived the hotel was crammed with journalists and Army officers, the latter bitterly critical of the British decision to halt their triumphant drive down the Suez Canal, in the face of opposition from the United States, almost as soon as they had landed.

I commiserated. Irrespective of the rights or wrongs of the initial decision to invade we had done it. We should, surely, have finished the job with a leonine roar instead of a miaow.

Again I observed the foreign correspondents from the wings as, prompt at 6 p.m., they presented themselves at the bar, freshly showered and elegant in light-weight suits having been flown across the Mediterranean from Port Said by the RAF.

And I discovered to my astonishment that, as the whisky sours and Keo beers were consumed — and signed for — the talk was more of the past than the exciting present. Korea, Mau Mau, Malaya. . . .

131

Even more disconcerting the correspondents lapsed from time to time into cablese. They wouldn't be driving to Kyrenia in the morning: they would be going *Kyreniawards*.

As in any representative gathering of any profession there were among them a few phonies; these preferred to gather their information in bars rather than battle-fields. Understandably they were pathologically insecure and viewed any determined exit from the bar with suspicion.

When I got up to leave on my first evening I was immediately stopped by an Englishman with a map of a river and its multitude of tributaries on his nose.

"Anything doing, old man?" he asked.

I stared him straight in his bloodshot eyes and said with aplomb: "Nothing that I know of. I'm merely going bog-wards."

*   *   *

On my second day in Nicosia, I became an accredited war correspondent. In common with the other correspondents I was given the honorary rank of captain, a bizarre promotion because I had been demobbed from the RAF with the rank of AC2 with the character reference *good* which is tantamount to being branded an incorrigible rogue.

I wore a peaked cap bearing a large gold letter C which was intended to stand for Correspondent, khaki shirt and trousers.

That morning I boarded an RAF transport plane and flew to Port Said, ostensibly to pick up my colleagues' copy and transmit it from Nicosia because communications from Egypt were hazardous, but determined to find a story of my own.

Beside me on the plane bucketing over the Mediterranean was the singer Lita Rosa on her way to entertain the troops.

She was a gorgeous, chirpy brunette, free-lancing after a sojourn with Joe Loss and his orchestra.

In my bachelor days I had coveted her from afar when she sang at the Hammersmith Palais. I discovered to my delight that I hadn't been wrong. She was gutsy, professional and delicious and wowed them in the shell-torn city of Port Said where the smell of explosives and death lingered heavily on the air.

Despite the ceasefire Egyptians were still sniping from rooftops and the destruction wreaked, as always, on an innocent population who knew as much about the machinations of Anthony Eden and Gamal Nasser as they did about the Theory of Relativity, was everywhere sickeningly apparent.

The walls of shattered buildings swayed and creaked in the breeze; homeless families loitered in bewildered groups awaiting the brusque kindliness of the Military; children wearing blood-stained bandages, still too young for bewilderment, searched for buried toys.

How many dead? How many maimed? And to what purpose?

So much for history books slyly glorifying misery; so much for authors masking their complexes with battle-cry prose.

Look upon a photograph of one child, born with trust, blinded or cripped by an exploding shell and any *cause* deemed worthy of sacrifice shrivels and dies.

Is it not time that cowardice took its rightful place in the assessment of human virtues? Right there alongside heroism?

I was taken around the crumbling, dun-coloured port in a military truck with a young Army PRO named Michael Parkinson. At the time I was asking all the questions; these days he asks all the questions, and to much more effect.

Later I wandered round the city by myself still in search of a story outside the scope of the correspondents who, with silk scarves at their necks and binoculars bumping against their chests, looked as though they were awaiting Rommel's next offensive.

Two of them, with commendable initiative, had established themselves in a brothel. Through a shell-hole in the wall they could be seen typing their stories attended by two buxom whores.

I spoke to several soldiers who, having appraised my uniform with baffled conjecture, treated me indulgently. They had one complaint in common: no beer.

Their plight was right up the *Mirror's* street and the story was prominently displayed the following day. And I like to think that, because of it, the troops got their wallop.

*   *   *

At first I made the trip to Port Said regularly. But, as the military campaign dragged towards its ignominious conclusion — the canal was blocked by Nasser, the Anglo-French forces withdrew and petrol rationing was re-introduced in Britain — I concentrated more on the anti-British terrorists in Cyprus seeking union with Greece.

The long-running tragedy — almost daily bombings and shootings — was heightened by the setting. Lemon groves, olive trees, spines of mountains flushed pink at dawn and dyed crimson at dusk, villages grouped around old men sipping treacle-thick coffee, the battlements of St. Hilarion on which Walt Disney was said to have modelled his castle for Snow White. . ..

The days were blue and gold, the air subtly iced with autumn.

Nicosia wasn't a handsome city but it possessed dusty charms, glimpses of ancient graces. And the bark of Sten guns in Ledra Street, known as Murder Mile, seemed barely to ruffle its air of historic assurance.

As the killers fled, as the blood was hosed from the street, the shops re-opened and laces and shawls fluttered from stalls like flags of truce.

British troops, Turkish policemen and civilians and suspected Greek-Cypriot traitors were the targets of the gunmen. And there was never much chance of eradicating them as they took refuge in the protective custody of their homes in the honeycombed streets of Nicosia, Limmasol, or Famagusta.

The leader of the terrorists was a wily tactician named Grivas who looked like the Hollywood actor Adolph Menjou. One news agency repeatedly reported that he had been captured; but he never was.

The Ledra Palace continued to serve the joint functions of military mess and Press Club and it was there that I first met the photographer Terry Fincher, then working for a picture agency.

Terry, a tough, barrel-chested Cockney who enjoys a good war as others enjoy a day at the races, arrived in Nicosia from Port Said, burned walnut-brown by the sun and stinking after an accidental dip in an Egyptian sewer.

He had lost his jacket so, keeping well to the leeward, I offered him my blazer which barely covered his chest and hung like a skirt around his thighs. Together we demolished a bottle of ouzo, the lethal Greek answer to arak, and forged a friendship witnessed years later by millions on *This Is Your Life*.

By the time of his television appearance Terry had completed a triumphant period on the *Daily Express*, been acclaimed Photographer of the Year several times, and embarked on a free-lance career which enabled him to choose his wars and, I suspect, ferment them.

Any sentiment engendered by the appearance of other guests who had featured in Terry's life was instantly destroyed as I strode into the glare of the studio lights.

Terry looked up and said: "Your flies are undone."

I then recounted an experience when, believing that we had caught a fearful tropical disease, we went to some hovel in India, optimistically described as a doctor's surgery, for preventative treatment.

The doctor, who also cast spells, produced a hyperdermic syringe with a needle like a rusty bayonet and told me to drop my trousers.

While bending low and steeling myself for the assault I heard the unmistakeable click of a camera shutter and realised that Terry had taken a low-profile shot of me.

Years later he published a photograph of a bomb crater in the Himalayan foothills. I believe to this day that it was a picture of my backside.

*   *   *

The difficulty with the EOKA campaign from the newspaperman's point of view was that, because of their frequency, the killings lost their impact. To make headlines a story had to be particularly poignant or feature some outstanding act of courage.

On November 29th, 1956, Mrs. Muriel Middleton, provided the courage. A formidable lady, Mrs. Middleton, aged thirty-six, stood at the door of her home in Limassol waving goodbye to her husband, Harry, a warrant officer in the Royal Army Service Corps. Their house was in Eleftheria Street, Limassol's Murder Mile. And Mrs. Middleton noticed two youths lounging near a lamp post.

As she shouted a warning to her husband one of the youths drew a gun and shot him in the back. Then Mrs. Middleton attacked. She rushed screaming at the youths who stood stunned like rabbits in the beams of a car's headlights. She managed to grab one but he came to life and leaped over a wall; the other fled down the street.

If Mrs. Middleton, mother of two, hadn't hurled herself at the gunmen then her husband would have been killed. As it was he escaped with a flesh-wound in the back. That was the sort of story one rejoiced to find.

The distressing aspect, futile bloodshed apart, was the age of so many of the terrorists. Young and malleable minds schooled to believe that shooting a man in the back was a heroic act of patriotism.

Like the teenagers in every country addled by terrorism they grew to accept violence and their characters were forever flawed by unscrupulous men who mobilised their innocence.

Not even girls were exempt.

I covered a court case when two beautiful shorthand typists,

136

both seventeen, were prosecuted for possessing and carrying arms.

They had been stopped in their small saloon car at a road-block. Sweet and demure they seemed. But in their handbags, amid the usual confusion of lipsticks and powder compacts, the security men found two bombs.

The girls were goaled for seven and two years respectively. An infinitely sad way to round off those transient, teenage years which should be reserved for dawning understanding and first love.

But in all the tragedies that sustain newspapers there are always glimpses of humour and compassion that confound cynicism. Mrs. Judith Doughty-Wylie, seventy-eight year old widow of a First World War VC, helped me to find one of those glimpses.

For eight years this silver-haired old lady had run a canteen for the British troops in the Suez Canal Zone. When the British pulled out she decided to move to the RAF base at Akrotiri, sixty miles from Nicosia.

Falling in with the spirit of the thing, the RAF air-lifted her home and kitchen, two metal sheds, from Suez to Cyprus. And there she dispensed bangers and beans and mugs of tea — 2½d a cuppa — to Servicemen driven from the NAAFI by pianists challenging anyone to "Come Back to Sorrento".

At first the officers at the base were worried for Mrs. Doughty-Wylie's safety. But they gave up worrying because, as one put it, "she's a bloodly sight tougher than us."

Her imperturbable spirit provided me with my second signed feature article in the *Mirror* and a welcome diversion from recording death.

On the rare occasions when there was a respite from the carnage we used to drive across the sun-baked plains and through the road-blocks to the little port of Kyrenia squatting at the foot of the mountains where the Crusaders once fought.

There we ate lobsters and steaks at the Harbour Club run by Judy Shirley, who once sang in a radio show called "Monday Night at Eight", and her husband. We gazed at the winter sea permed with white waves and besported ourselves in the manner of troops relaxing behind the front line.

Except that there wasn't any established front-line and when we drove back gunfire would crackle in the hills. Fortified by Cyprus wine and brandy, we would assure each other that, through their binoculars, the gunmen would undoubtedly see the Press cards displayed on the windscreen.

This, the first of my many visits to Cyprus, ended just before Christmas. Ken Hord, always acutely aware of the strains imposed on family life by the demands of a reporter's profession, recalled me for the festivities.

And for the first time I became aware of the great bonus of foreign assignments. The return. Cockney voices at the airport, the first pint of bitter, the casual sanity of the Anglo-Saxon, the humour based on an innate sense of the ridiculous which no other nation possesses.

Dot Watson greeted me emotionally as though I had been riddled with bullets. Ken Hord shook my firmly by the hand, a giddy accolade.

At a party in Mitcham I encountered the attitude experienced by every journalist coming home from foreign parts: total indifference to the hazards you have been through.

"So, where have you been to?" someone down the road asked.

"Suez," I said and watching his eyes glaze, I *heard* him think: "Lambert's bull-shitting again."

When the next guest inquired where I had been hiding myself I said: "Resting," leaving him with the comfortable impression that I had spent the last three months in Wormwood Scrubs.

XVI

Any hopes I had harboured that I was now fit to join the ranks of the Sefton Delmers and Noel Barbers of journalism were soon confounded.

My successes had, after all, only been modest and I now found myself involved in the spirit of clubbiness that was pervading Fleet Street. Newspapers were seeking to spread a sense of cameraderie among their readers by enrolling them in common endeavour.

The *Mirror* was pioneering the hula-hoop craze and, through some monstrous misunderstanding, I was dispatched to the Hammersmith Palais to demonstrate the pelvic arts of this pastime.

Never strong on athletic prowess — at school I had managed to break my arm skipping — I was propelled protesting hysterically in front of a bevy of nubile girls expectantly awaiting a lesson from the master.

It all seemed a far cry from the shell-pocked city of Port Said as, whimpering softly, I took off my jacket, stepped into a bloody great hoop and stood transfixed in the middle of the ballroom.

From the wings came the irritated voice of a promotions executive. "For God's sake get on with it man."

I gyrated my hips vigorously and the hoop fell to the floor.

"That's how not to do it," the man from promotions said brightly apparently convinced that I had done this on purpose.

Once more I waggled my hips like some male belly-dancer in a dubious club in Tangier. Once more the hoop fell to the ground as though drawn by an invisible magnet.

"And now the real thing," intoned the optimistic fool in the background.

This time the hoop remained around my midrift for a couple of whirls but I found to my alarm that my trousers were beginning to fall down.

My dilemma was agonising. I had for the first, and probably only, time managed to retain the hoop round my hips; if I stopped gyrating then it would fall once more; if I didn't stop then my trousers would, and I would be escorted to the police station accused of indecent exposure.

I was saved from making the crucial decision by a stab of pain in my back. I allowed the hoop to drop, grabbed my trousers and limped away from the bewildered gaze of my pupils.

God knows what happened in the Palais after that because I hobbled away and caught a bus home. A doctor told me that I had put my sacro-iliac out but it was nothing compared to the dislocation of my ego.

But my most alarming club experience involved an association of the fattest women in Britain who had banded together to project and share the joys and sorrows of excessive adipose tissue.

It was decided to fly three of the largest down to Woburn Abbey, ancestral home of the publicity-conscious Duke of Bedford, and I was appointed guardian.

If I had known that it was proposed to fly them by helicopter I might have feigned illness. Alas, I had no idea that some inspired ideas maniac had opted for a whirly-bird; nor had I any idea of quite how enormous the ladies were.

Together they must have weighed more than sixty stone. Standing on its pad in the morning sun, the helicopter looked decidedly frail.

I asked the pilot, himself no lightweight, what the maximum permitted load was but he said he didn't know. "We only go by the number of passengers."

"But we've got the equivalent of more than six passengers there," I pointed out.

"Ah well," he said, "it's not far to fall."

The ladies, all exuberantly cheerful, climbed into the contraption and I squeezed in beside them. The photographer had craftily arranged to meet us at Woburn Abbey.

"This is better than Southend," one of the ladies confided.

"What's better?" I asked.

"I wanted to go on one of those joy-flights but the pilot couldn't get the plane off the ground. Blamed me, ruddy cheek."

I wondered what made her think this pilot was going to get off the ground.

But he did. He coaxed the great dragonfly into the air and set off on course for Woburn Abbey.

The ladies chatted away eagerly pointing out objects of interest unaware that — or so it seemed to me — the machine lurched closer to the ground every time they moved. I knew that journalists were insured by their offices when they flew; I was unsure whether any policy covered the force of gravity applied to 840 pounds of female flesh.

The ordeal was mitigated to an extent by the personalities of my fellow travellers. They had heard all the jokes about their size; they didn't give a damn and they were out to enjoy themselves. And they certainly weren't going to let my lugubrious presence — "You're just a bag of bones, boyo" — spoil their day.

At last the helicopter settled in front of the magnificent building and we climbed out. The pilot, I noticed, had shed his breezy nonchalance and was shaking and wiping the sweat from his forehead.

We spent a pleasant day at the Abbey and I telephoned a story. Just before we were due to leave I perpetrated an act of craven cowardice.

"Aren't you coming with us?" one of them asked.

I shook my head. "I live out this way." And with a smirk as

false as an election promise I turned on my heel and set out on foot for the railway station.

Fan clubs also provided a fair amount of footage for newspapers and sometimes, particularly on bleak Sundays — stories lacking immediacy were often held marked *Sun. for Mon.* — news-starved editors enrolled the support of these organisations.

I once travelled to a seaside resort to wine and dine selected members of the Mario Lanza Fan Club who had been competing to prove who had attended the most of the chubby tenor's movies. One of them had seen *The Great Caruso* sixty-two times.

On another occasion it was decided to hold a reception for a fan club from the north with the object of their adoration, a male pop star with a voice so weak that he practically had to swallow the microphone to be heard, in attendance.

The club was expected at Euston Station at 5.30 p.m. on a wintry evening and I was deputed with a photographer to meet them.

The train arrived on time and we searched the hurrying crowds for the placards, the rosettes, the banners proclaiming WE LOVE ERNIE (that wasn't his name but it's kinder to disguise his true identity).

The crowd dispersed. No fan club. One man wearing a raincoat fashioned for someone twice his height was left standing on the platform. From beneath the raincoat protruded shoes split at the seams like over-ripe pomegranates; his hair was larded over his head and one of the lenses of his steel-framed spectacles was seamed with cracks.

I approached him cautiously and asked him if he had seen any of the fan club when he embarked on the train.

"I am the fan club," he said, a note of menace in his voice.

"What do you mean you're the fan club?"

"Just what I told thee lad, I'm bloody fan club."

"But we had a letter. . . ."

"Aye, I wrote bugger."

"Where are all the other members then?"

142

"Letter didn't say owt about numbers did it?" One eye glared at me through the unbroken lens.

"You mean you're the only member?"

"Aye, I'm chairman and secretary too. Now come on lad, I haven't come all this way to chew fat with thee. I want to see our lad."

"*Your* lad," I reminded him.

I whispered to the photographer. "He's all yours."

"Oh no he bloody isn't," the photographer said.

"Well keep him chatting while I 'phone the office."

The Fan Club stared at us suspiciously. "What's going on? Am I going to get to see our lad or aren't I? You promised, you know. . . ."

"Of course you are," I said. "Our lad — your lad — is dying to meet you."

Not only that, I thought, but he'll finally swallow the microphone if he sets eyes on you.

The photographer said: "I'm off."

"For God's sake help out."

"Cost you a pint."

"Make it a Scotch," I said and raced for the telephone.

When I reported that the Fan Club consisted of one lunatic there was a shocked silence at the other end of the phone.

Then a voice said: "What are you going to do about it, old boy? We've laid on a buffet."

"No," I said, "what are *you* going to do about it?"

I heard a muffled conversation and some exclamations of consternation. Then the news desk assistant came back to me. "Get rid of him. Tell him Ernie's ill. Pay him off."

"How much?"

"Give him a fiver and see how it goes. If he's awkward make it a tenner."

The phone went dead.

I told the Fan Club that Ernie was suffering from measles and offered him £5 for his trouble.

The Fan Club regarded the note in bewilderment. "Is this for me?"

143

"For you and all the other members."

"A fiver?"

"Aye," I said, "a fiver. Here make it a tenner." I borrowed another note from the aggrieved photographer and handed it to him.

"A tenner? Bloody 'eck lad. I've never had so much ackers in my life."

He stuffed the notes in the pocket of his extraordinary raincoat. "Tell you what, I'm off up West End now. Find myself a nice piece of stuff maybe." One eye winked behind the good lens. "And as for that Ernie. Always thought he was a big-headed bugger at best of times."

*   *   *

From time to time we also had to attend various beauty contests. Miss British Railways, Miss Smithfield Market — Miss Conduct as we called them.

The assignments were usually fruitless as far as the reporter was concerned because all he had to do was supply a caption to a toothpaste smile, a sash across a swimming costume and a pair of gorgeous legs in high-heeled shoes. Attempting to invest these occasions with newsworthiness was as hopeless as trying to alter the phraseology of a weather story.

However it was pleasant to relax watching the lovelies parading up and down the platform and giving reign to the fantasies that assail men on such occasions.

Often relatives and friends were present. On one occasion a grey-haired woman with a brolly firmly clenched between her knees was visibly upset by the judges' choice of a girl other than her daughter. Her daughter was runner-up.

"More to it here than meets the eye," she muttered, practically snapping the handle of her umbrella. "Wonder what that young hussy did to get the chairman on her side."

Something pretty spectacular, I thought, because the chairman of the judges was senile and twice had to be woken up as the lovely creatures floated past him.

144

I moved away not wanting to be in contact with the umbrella if the runner-up's mother suddenly went out of control.

I chatted with some of the organisers and one of them confided that she thought the winner was wearing a waspie, a tiny corset. "Strictly speaking it's against the rule," she said. "But there's not much we can do about it."

I had never since my arrival in Fleet Street manufactured stories. But I could see no objection to activating facts.

I returned to the woman with the umbrella, sat down beside her and said: "You've got to admit she's a pretty girl."

"Who's a pretty girl?" fingers tightening on the umbrella handle.

"The girl who won."

"That hussy? We all know what she is, don't we."

"I suppose it was the waspie that helped," I said.

"The what?"

"The waspie."

"You mean she was stung by a waspie?"

I explained what a waspie was.

"And she's wearing one?"

"So I believe."

I expected a protest but wasn't prepared for what ensued. The grey-haired woman leaped to her feet, charged across the stage and prodded the smiling winner in her navel with the point of her umbrella.

"True or false," she bellowed.

The poor girl backed away but the point of the umbrella followed her remorselessly. "Come on, out with it, true or false."

From either side agitated officials were moving in on the runner-up's mother but she turned, scattering them with a scything movement of her brolly, shouting: "She's an imposter."

Then she returned to her victim, pinning her in the stomach like Douglas Fairbanks Jnr. with a rapier at the throat of a fallen rival.

145

"Out with it," she bellowed. "Are you wearing a beezie or aren't you?"

"Isn't that what guardsmen wear on their heads?" someone said.

By this time the female organisers had managed to pinion the umbrella-wielding woman's arms.

"But I tell you she's wearing a beezie."

"Do you mean a waspie?"

"A corset."

"Ah." One of the women turned to the winner. "Are you wearing a waspie?"

"Of course I'm not," the wretched girl protested.

"Oh yes she is." Another prod with the umbrella which seemed to have encountered something more solid than flesh in the region of the girl's midriff.

"Oh no I'm not." The girl who was as tough as she was lissom grasped the umbrella and thrust it back at the enraged matron who collapsed in a flurry of petticoats and other articles of underwear which neither beauty queen nor runner-up would have dreamed of wearing.

Then, watched by horrified officials, the two joined battle encouraged by shouts and war-whoops from the hitherto demure contestants. When they were finally parted the waistline of the newly-crowned queen was a curious shape.

The flushed girl adjusted the twisted waspie and philosphically acknowledged defeat. And for once a minor beauty contest was accorded more than a caption beneath a couple of shapely legs.

XVII

I was often advised to specialise. In crime, industrial relations, science, politics. . . .

But specialisation wasn't for me. The great dividend of journalism was the daily contact with characters as diverse as rat-catchers or Royalty. The taking of life's pulse.

Specialise and you forfeited that dividend. You slotted yourself in a niche where every day you met the same clients. Could anything be more melancholy than regularly meeting politicians?

When the general news reporter arrived in the office he might be dispatched to interview a road sweeper — in fact I was once because he owned a Rolls-Royce — a gangster or a Cabinet minister.

What's more it was always futile to anticipate their reactions to a visit from the Press. A film star who had clambered to the top through a series of publicity stunts could do a Garbo on you: a notoriously reticent diplomat could suddenly contact verbal diarrhoea.

Montgomery, for instance. I was sent to his country home to seek his reaction to some controversial views expressed by an American general on military strategy in World War II.

I expected some snapping reprimand. "Straighten yourself up there, laddie. When did you last have your hair cut?" The least I could expect, I speculated, would be a week's jankers.

Instead he showed me round his garden, mildly observed that the general was talking balderdash and agreed to pose for a photograph with me. The picture still stands on my mother's television set.

But what, I wondered, would be the reactions of Arthur Askey, the diminutive comedian, when I asked him if he knew he had been "a murder suspect".

A thirty-six year-old woman, Mrs. Diana Suttey, had been strangled in a lane near Hemel Hempstead and police were searching for the driver of a light-coloured car with a registration number beginning SUU or SUV. The driver was said to be small with hair greying at the temples, an oval-shaped face and wearing horn-rimmed glasses with thick lenses.

I had a drink with a detective who casually mentioned that Arthur Askey had been interviewed. The reaction of the news desk to this information was far from casual. They expected one of the routine developments — police finger-printing the whole town or the scene re-enacted one month later. . . .

Instead Lambert — hadn't he been involved in some farcical incident with a dog in the office? — had come up with the preposterous suggestion that the cheerful, pint-sized comic had been questioned.

A cold voice asked: "Have you been drinking?"

"No," I lied.

Silence. Then with ponderous sarcasm: "I suppose Stinker Murdoch has been interviewed too?"

"No," I said. "Nor has Cheerful Charlie Chester. But Arthur Askey has."

"Who says so?"

"A copper," I said.

"Was he sloshed?"

"No," I said with dignity, "he wasn't." But the alarming possibility that he had been joking now occurred to me.

"Have you got quotes to back it up?"

"Not yet."

"Then you'd better get them, old man. And they'd better be good."

Filled with foreboding I telephoned Big-hearted Arthur at his flat in Kensington. Immediately the chirpy voice confirmed that he had been interviewed. I leaned against the door of the telephone kiosk as my blood began to circulate again.

He was, of course, one of thousands of men answering the description who had been questioned. And he had a fawn car with a registration number beginning SUU or SUV.

At the time of the murder he had been in a show at Torquay and was promptly eliminated from police inquiries. "But it was a bit of a shock all the same," he told me.

Next day the story was the back-page lead with my byline above a thumbnail photograph of Arthur Askey. As a child I had always loved him on the radio show *Bandwagon*; that day I idolised him.

But what if he'd said: "No comment"?

*   *   *

Politicians are among the most difficult subjects to interview because they have perfected the art of not answering questions and doing it at considerable length.

The bereaved, as I have said, are often the easiest because they want to share their grief.

Sportsmen can be difficult, particularly if they've just fallen off a horse, been convicted of drunkenness or missed a crucial penalty.

Heavyweight boxers should only be approached by telephone as a colleague on the *Mirror* discovered. He waylaid a pugilist in a country lane and was punched through the hedge.

Clergymen can be elusive, as a photographer on the *Daily Express*, discovered. He opened the boot of a car and discovered a vicar for whom the Press had been searching, curled up inside. His photograph of the foetal-like man of God hung in the *Express* newsroom for many years and perhaps still does.

Personally I found the young men and women trying to imitate the thoroughbreds of Society the most difficult to interview. They were mostly impecunious, on the make and aware in rare moments of honest introspection that they would never really be accepted.

149

They lived in dingy rooms just outside the acceptable limits of Knightsbridge, Chelsea and Kensington; they drank at the Markham and the Chelsea Potter where reluctantly they bought the occasional drink; they bought elegant suits on the never-never; they were forever recovering from some bash and they referred to "Liz and Maggie" as though they lived next door.

Such were their raging complexes that they reacted facetiously to any questioning. Their banalities raised a titter in the presence of other fringe products but when they were recorded in cold print they gave the game away and further insulated their authors from the *crème de la crème*.

Standing in Barney Finnegans one day, I was perusing with a girl reporter a picture adorning a story I had written about some escapade involving this breed.

"Don't they look a lot of worms," she observed. "Just look at them," prodding the photograph with her finger.

"An absolute shower," I agreed. "The whole lot of them."

On closer inspection I discovered that one of the "worms" was Derek Lambert who had inadvertently got himself into the picture.

*   *   *

Although journalistically my career was proceeding satisfactorily the same could hardly be said about my personal public relations.

It was the custom when compiling a story in the office to telephone a local correspondent, enlist his help and make sure that the newsdesk put him on the daily list for payment. When I first joined the *Mirror* I was inclined to be power-mad. Never before had I been in a position of such authority.

One bitter, snow-filled night I called an alert free-lance named Ferrari in Dartford, Kent, and told him to proceed forthwith and get some quotes from one of the protagonists in the story I was writing. Ferrari said he was suffering from a severe cold and would I mind, in view of the arctic weather, if he got the quotes by phone.

Indignantly I drew myself up into a posture of bristling indignation and thundered down the phone: "Just get out there Ferrari," and hung up.

Not long afterwards Dan Ferrari, a jovial, heavily-moustached extrovert, was appointed deputy night news editor and was subsequently further elevated in the editorial hierarchy.

On another bleak night when a snow-flecked wind was whistling across London from Siberia he asked me to do a door-step job, — hang around someone's front-door until they either arrived or departed.

I may have taken an undue time putting on my overcoat because from behind the newsdesk he suddenly exploded: "Just get out there, Lambert," and grinned with the satisfaction which he fully deserved.

On another occasion I was asked to take under my wing for a day a new reporter. Knowing just how he was feeling I did my best to acquaint him with office procedures.

Together we did the chores. Searched trade magazines for stories, perused the *London Gazette* which was delivered at about 6 p.m., obtained non-committal quotes from various ministries and read the Parliamentary questions.

The latter task was really a back-up operation in case any devastating questions had been missed by the political reporters. Once I did unearth a gem — an M.P. asking whether steps could be taken to raise the height of the roofs of London taxis because every time he climbed into a cab his bowler hat fell off.

My relationship with the new arrival proceeded pleasantly enough until in the evening we adjourned to Barney Finnegans for a few baptismal pints. There, after the third pint, we embarked upon a bitter argument that progressed inexorably from politics to religion to personal abuse.

I must have made some particularly offensive remark because, with a hoarse cry, my protégé suddenly snatched his tankard from the bar and hurled its contents in my direction. I ducked and a high-ranking executive entering the bar received the beer full in his face.

He stood there for a moment with a puzzled frown on his face because, although the bar was famous for the speed of its service, his arrival on this occasion seemed to have been anticipated with uncanny precision.

He took his pipe from his mouth and poured beer and soggy ashes from it. Then, shaking his head, he made his way to the bar where I heard him asking a subordinate: "Who is that young man?"

"God knows," said the subordinate.

"Then find out."

My fledgling charge stared at me with an expression in which reproach, hatred and despair were inextricably mixed. I had to admit that it was hardly an auspicious beginning to a career in Fleet Street.

There was only one thing for it.

I approached the dripping executive and, in a rambling bumble of words, explained what had happened.

At the end of it the executive said: "And who, pray, are you?"

I told him; he seemed unimpressed. My name, however, had sunk home because for the next three weeks I was given the late, late shift.

And as for my protégé, he prospered with a spate of bylined stories which I read with mixed feelings at four in the morning in the company of the office cleaners.

*   *   *

Suicides were the most deeply disturbing events we covered; more so than disasters where one's faculties were blunted by the immensity of the tragedy. But at inquests the coroner's verdict that a man or women took his or her life "while of unsound mind" explained nothing, and as I walked from those impersonal, oak-panelled chambers and smelled the fresh air

152

as a man smells it after a long illness, and heard bird-song, the despair of the dead reached out and touched me.

I covered many inquests, plane and rail crashes but these are outside the mood of this book. In fact even the following sequence is a little morbid: the reader preferring his gin without bitters would be well advised to skip it.

The police, at that time, had been receiving too much unfavourable publicity and it was decided that it would somehow dispel some of this by opening up Limehouse police station for the public; the reasoning was as obtuse as many of the pre-war mystery stories set in that area.

There stood Chinatown before it moved during the war to Liverpool. There prowled Dr. Fu Manchu; there stood Thomas Burke staring into the swirling mist and wreathing stories about the almond-eyes that stared back. There Jack the Ripper wet his lips and sharpened his knife as the tarts drifted past in the choking fog.

I toured the police station with a group of housewives and children and one or two old customers while a policeman resentfully led us around pointing out the exhibits like a guide in a museum.

We saw the charge room, bare and clean and hopeless, with a desk and a chair and measurements on the walls for sizing up clients. We visited the cells, white-tiled like bathless bathrooms. I imagined the drunks awakening there, trying to remember, repenting, swearing never to touch another drop; or the alcoholics unshaven and dishevelled, disjointed minds crying for more liquor.

"All centrally-heated," our guide grudgingly told us. "The drunks like it here. Get quite stroppy if they're carted off to another nick."

We were shown the finger-printing equipment, a murder bag and, outside, police horses and dogs and a Daimler Dart sports car for chasing the ton-up boys.

The policemen were all elaborately polite like teachers on Parents' Day and we were given no hint of the desperate and squalid scenes that must have been enacted here. Nevertheless, on emerging I experienced the same sense of relief that assailed me the day I was demobbed.

XVIII

The social life of reporters was pretty much of a closed shop.

In the pubs strangers from other walks of life were greeted cordially and then edged to the fringe of the conversation and company. There was no churlish intent: it was merely that we were so incestuously occupied with our calling that the gossip and escapades involving other professions interested us little. We did, after all, spend every working day recording their achievements and their frailties.

No one went straight home. We stopped at Barney Finnegans or the Printer's Devil or one of the neutral Fleet Street pubs as inevitably as a train bound for southern suburbs stops at Clapham Junction.

Then, spirits emboldened by a few draughts of Mieux's bitter or Flower's Keg, we moved into foreign territory because no one could accuse us of lobbying for jobs on other papers if we entered their pubs mob-handed.

The Mucky Duck, the Feathers, the Falstaff, the Punch, Aunty's. . . . Some of the braver souls even gate-crashed Poppins, the hallowed drinking quarters of the *Daily Express*.

Beer gave way to shorts and the £3 cajoled from the news desk in lieu of expenses dwindled to a handful of loose coins. "Time please. . . . Come on, gentlemen, it's ten minutes after time. . . ." We supped up and stood miserably in the street somewhere between Ludgate Circus and the Law Courts debating whom we would honour with a request to cash a cheque for a quid.

Some of us adjourned to Harry Greens, a West End night

club with a floor show and a friendly disposition towards the Press; others called at the Press Club where, in the bar adorned with cartoonists' impressions of the more distinguished members, the cheques mounted up in direct ratio to the amount of booze consumed.

For the select few who owned cars the dilemma then was to drive or not to drive. One night Hugh Saker, a Falstaffian character who saw more than most with his one eye, solved the problem by telephoning his wife at their home in Addington, Surrey, and asking her to come and collect him.

His conscious assuaged, he then disposed of several large Scotches while his wife Vivien Bachelor, a vivacious brunette who worked on the *Evening Standard*, motored through the night.

Hugh was poured into the car by other reporters who noted that his wife was wearing only a night-dress. Half way home Vivien was caught short, stopped the car and disappeared into a field.

Whereupon Hugh woke up with a start and, having forgotten that he had summoned his wife to the rescue, decided that he must have stopped for a snooze. He moved over to the driving seat, started the engine and finished the journey alone.

He was only faintly surprised to find that Vivien wasn't at home — newspapers have a habit of dispatching reporters on stories at the dead of night — and took himself to bed where he fell instantly asleep.

While he snored peacefully his wife, several miles away, was trying to explain to a patrolling policeman how she came to be in a field at 2 a.m. wearing only her nightdress.

*   *   *

The conviviality was often merely a continuation of the working day.

The pub was office, confessional and, on out-of-town stories, home. Locations were automatically linked by the office with their hostelries; if you were at the Old Bailey then the switchboard called you at the Stump and Magpie; if you were at the Law Courts they tried the George; if you were attending the Disciplinary Committee of the General Medical Council they telephoned two pubs off Hallam Street where actors from the BBC rehearsed their lines in between bites of cheese sandwiches.

The reliance on pubs didn't mean that we were all habitual drunkards: pubs were a necessary part of our lives. Where else would you meet a detective who was about to nick the prime suspect but in the pub? Where else could you write a story, gobble a snack and use the landlord's telephone to dictate your copy? Where else could you give the office a contact number and await their queries over a pint? Certainly not in a Lyon's tea-shop.

When the Press took to a pub the landlord's future prosperity was assured provided he didn't offend in some subtle way. I have seen Press pubs packed one day with regulars, deserted the next. Often the publican had no idea what crime he had perpetrated; sometimes we weren't too sure either.

The calculated gamble the publican had to take was whether or not to cash cheques. He also had to accept that his telephone would be in constant use and that, when it rang, a degree of diplomacy was required — "Are you here or not?" to a reporter who was manifestly there with a light-ale in his hand.

Pubs served one other purpose rarely acknowledged: they were havens where we could purge vicarious grief. There is really nowhere else to go on a hostile night after you have listened to details of torture inflicted on a child by its parents, stood outside prison walls while a man is executed, picked a little girl's doll from the wreckage of an aircraft. . . .

I covered the inquest of a promising young scientist who had taken an overdose of drugs because he had failed an examination. He was an only child and he left behind middle-aged parents who had forged their life around him. Now there was no future and the past was merely the foundations of hopelessness.

I covered the court martial of an Army officer who had

157

given his life to the military; when, so he believed, he was ostracised in the officers' mess because he had come up through the ranks he tried to take his life by slashing his wrists. He was dismissed the Service.

After chronicling such events I adjourned, with the cold fingers of futility pressing my temples, to the nearest tavern. Drowned other people's sorrows with a pint and, glass of whisky in hand, waited until I heard again children's laughter and saw lights reflected on the baubles of a Christmas tree.

Social activities on days off were limited. Principally by shortage of cash — neither house nor furniture was paid for — and the arrival of a brother for Patrick, a curly-haired charmer whom we called Martin Nicholas.

If we went out for a drink in the winter we had to sit in leafless pub gardens with the cherry-nosed children swathed in clothes like Bonfire Night guys; if spring beckoned us to the cushions of the North Downs we had to travel by Green Line coach.

Finally, after a £2 a week rise, I risked bankruptcy by buying a small, red second-hand car on hire purchase. After twelve driving lessons I passed the test despite stalling the car in Wimbledon High Street.

We celebrated by driving one Sunday in March to Horsham. There were still wings of snow in the fields and on high ground, where it lay in thick quilts, it was shadowed with zebra-stripes by tall trees.

But I was mobile and free. There were fresh, clean smells abroad; snowdrops pirouetted in gardens; last summer's leaves rustled in the gutters. For two months the countryside had been imprisoned in white amber; today it was coming to life, and us with it.

We had a drink at a pub called the Star in Rusper complete with an inglenook, lots of copper and voices as ripe as old cheese, and lunched at a Trust House in Horsham which reminded me of a setting in a John Braine novel: two Jaguars outside, three fur coats inside, studied weekend clothes and Dover sole for 10s.6d.

I drove back along roads crowded with emergent hikers, cyclists and cars. By 4 p.m. there was almost a summer languor in the air; by five it had been frozen once more and we were reminded that spring was still three weeks away. Those were the sort of mellow intermissions that I enjoyed while helping to keep the daily diary of strangers.

At the same time I was also experiencing considerable stress because I was trying to stop smoking. I got through sixty a day and had decided, when the price was increased by 1d. a packet, that it was foolhardy to spend all that lovely money on something that certainly wasn't doing my health any good. Hollywood reporters spent much of their time lighting cigarettes and immediately squashing them with a finality that boded ill for the corrupt sheriff or financier.

I decided that a new image should be forged for reporters. No more cigarettes wagging in the corner of the mouth during an interview, no more ash scattered, Hannen Swaffer style, over the suit, no more gut-wrenching coughs creased over the wash-basin in the morning.

My allies in the fight were peppermints and boasts. Every time I wanted a smoke, which was often, I sucked a mint; whenever I was in company I arrogantly proclaimed that I had conquered the foul habit with ease.

In fact, after a cup of tea or a glass of beer I was consumed with desire for the weed and at night I used to awake sweating, believing that I had lit up. Sometimes on the morning after a party I awoke with a renewed craving. Had alcohol weakened my resolve during the hooley? I was never quite sure.

However I persevered and haven't smoked a cigarette since that harrowing period. I can be unbearably pompous on the subject but do sincerely believe that it is tragic to see young people smoking because they wrongly believe it is the thing to do, bankrupting their pockets and possibly devastating their lives.

Life was further complicated at this time by my decision not to wait until middle-age to embark on a literary career.

For months I sat in a small, cold bedroom overlooking the

open-plan, pygmy-sized front gardens of the estate typing away with two numb fingers. I schooled myself to walk *past* Barney Finnegans; I closed my ears to the roars of the crowds at Tooting and Mitcham football ground and turned down the television in the lounge; I sacrificed days-off and became a morose, introverted bore.

The result was a novel entitled *In Our Time* based on my experiences at Suez. It consisted of 80,000 words of idealistic rubbish and was firmly rejected by six distinguished publishing houses.

Subsequently, having found refuge and balm behind the hedgerows and haystacks of Laurie Lee's childhood in *Cider With Rosie*, I decided that autobiography was my forte. But what had I to offer to compare with his descriptions of rural England being awoken by the fumes and reverberations of internal combustion? Certainly what I didn't have was his ability to strike exquisite chords of memory.

But I did have a war.

Once again I took to the bedroom and peered down a corridor of mirrors to my childhood during the Second World War. I called the book *The Shrapnel Days* because, instead of stamps, we collected shining splinters of shell casing, fragments from wrecked aircraft and the occasional unexploded incendiary bomb.

I sent the manuscript to Hutchinsons who enthused, suggested revisions and then rejected it. I then took it to André Deutsch who published it under the title *The Sheltered Days*. It was serialised on *Woman's Hour* on BBC radio accompanied by perky war-time melodies.

Not that it did me much good in Fleet Street. Members of the Hairy-Arsed Mob were not supposed to stray into Bohemia.

*   *   *

In any case I didn't want to depart the ranks of the hard news reporters; they saw far more of life than any feature writer or specialist. A week's stint at the Old Bailey or the General Medical Council and I had the seeds of half a dozen novels that might one day take root and blossom.

Unlike the other dailies, the *Mirror* in those days didn't have a permanent Old Bailey man and, when a likely case was about to open, one of us was plucked from the day shift and sent by foot to the awesome courthouse on the site of Newgate Prison.

Big trials following well-publicised murder investigations, or cases involving notorious villains or well-known personalities, were reported daily. Lesser cases with colourful backgrounds were barely touched upon so that a composite story could be produced on conviction.

Apart from actual court-reporting the essence of the job was collating background material and a guilty plea from the dock echoed as a cry of joy in the reporter's soul because he could then state evidence and background as fact without much fear of contradiction.

The periods when court reporters displayed most of the symptoms of imminent nervous breakdown came between the retirement and return of the jury. They prowled the bleak corridors of the Bailey, crossed the road to the Magpie and Stump for medicinal recuperatives, wrote and rewrote their intros.

The suspense often lasted for hours, sometimes continuing overnight. The longer the adjournment, according to the old-hands, the greater the possibility of an acquittal. Hope burgeoned in the breasts of those reporters who had confidently predicted a not-guilty verdict to their news editors: those who had staked their reputation on a conviction took themselves more frequently to the Stump.

The death penalty was still in force and the tension in the famous No. 1 Court — drop that "famous" at your peril — was palpable as the jury filed back and the prisoner emerged from the bowels of the building into the dock.

"Guilty, my lord."

A sigh of shared horror shivered in the air. Agency reporters

161

gathered at the doorway raced to the telephones in the Press room. The rest of us lingered in the Press bench for the macabre rituals invoked when a man was to be murdered for the crime of murder.

While the judge donned his black cap you gazed with horrified fascination at the man whose life was soon to be taken, recorded his reactions while your thoughts vaulted ahead to the condemned cell before stalling at the scaffold.

Those scenes convinced me that capital punishment was as heinous as murder; although I have modified my views in the instance of terrorists who indiscriminately slaughter innocents.

Visits to the disciplinary committee of the General Medical Council were usually fruitful because the public liked reading about susceptible doctors.

The reason was, I suppose, that doctors had for so long been pompously secretive about what was wrong with you. It never seemed to occur to them that it was *your* body they were talking about.

"Is it very bad, doctor?"

"Mmm," scribbling a sinister prescription.

"Is it contagious?"

"Just take it easy for a couple of weeks."

And then the question that really enraged them. "Doctor, what *is* the matter with me?"

"Nothing to worry about! Keep taking the tablets, next patient please."

The worst of the breed was personified by the family doctor in the movies who lingered outside the bedroom where the star's wife had just been in raucous labour.

Husband, hands locked in prayer: "Yes doctor?"

A long, sadistic pause, and then: "She's going to be all right, my boy."

"And the baby?"

Another long pause before the knowing smile begins to dawn. "It's a boy."

What did he expect, a St. Bernard?

With such attitudes abroad people adored reading about doctors' indiscretions.

If they were caught taking drugs or sniffing their own anaesthetics, driving drunkenly, advertising their services or carrying out illegal abortions then up they came before the disciplinary committee. But, of course, the offence which really rivetted attention on the 8.15 a.m. from Penge was misconduct with a woman patient.

Sometimes the doctors were guilty of betraying the Hippocratic oath; sometimes the poor fellows were guilty only of being physically attractive to a lusty housewife and being naive enough to examine her without a witness.

It must have been particularly galling for a doctor to hear his accuser shame-facedly reciting his misdeeds in a barely audible whisper when, at their last meeting, the surgery had rung with her climactic bellows of ecstasy. If, that is, her story was to be believed.

In many cases a patient's advances had been spurned and, in a jealous rage, she had confessed all to her husband dozing in his carpet slippers beside the fire. He was then persuaded to report the doctor — "Don't you care that your wife's honour has been tarnished?"

From the dais the doctors sitting in judgement listened pitilessly to the tales, true and false, of human fallibility. Unless the case against the doctor was patently a pack of lies he stood little chance of acquittal. A period of probation was about the best he could hope for; more often than not his name was struck off the medical register and his life ruined.

The magisterial doctors all looked pretty affluent and cold-blooded and it seemed to me wrong that such men, who would have clinically examined the apple in the Garden of Eden instead of eating it, should have been in a position to damn their more impoverished and hot-blooded colleagues.

The scenes in the street after a doctor had been acquitted or struck off were rumbustious. Reporters beseeched the doctors for quotes and followed them until they managed to escape by taxi. Their wives usually announced that they were going to

163

stick by their husbands, although their expressions contra-
dicted these avowals of loyalty and I often suspected that, after
they had got hubby home, it wouldn't be long before he
would have to seek medical treatment from one of his more
fortunate brethren.

Bankruptcy courts, I assumed, would be a dismal experience. Far from it. I discovered that it was only the honest,
small-time toilers of the world who feared insolvency and
regarded it as a disgrace: the fat cats who blandly agreed with
the Official Receiver that their life styles had been excessive
walked out of the old building in Carey Street with a new
spring to their step.

Bankruptcy, it seemed, was an accepted stratagem of big
business. A legitimate device to dissipate debts and repay them
in piffling instalments.

"But doesn't this mean you can't get credit?" I asked one
sleek financier when we adjourned to the Star down the street.
He choked over his large Scotch and, clutching his well-
nourished tummy heaving with merriment beneath his
immaculate double-breasted suit, spluttered: "Priceless. Absolutely priceless. Bit of a wag, aren't you. What are you having?"

The drawback to bankruptcy proceedings as far as I was
concerned was that only rarely could I understand what was
going on. I appreciated that skuttled fortunes, preposterous
frauds and, sometimes, broken dreams and withered hopes,
were being sorted into profits and losses, distilled into
deficiencies. But that was about all; when I stared at the actual
figures they stared back inscrutably. Luckily the courts
weren't far from the office and I could always scurry back and
crib the agency versions.

Among those who passed through the bankruptcy courts
were many actors who had been type-cast by television.
Among them the delightfully modest Bruce Seton who played
Fabian of the Yard in a long-running TV series.

Because, whether he subsequently played a defrocked vicar
or a Spanish nobleman, he was still Fabian to the viewers, he

164

got fewer and fewer parts and eventually went broke. Happily I attended his *discharge* from bankruptcy.

Ill health had been mentioned in court. Said Seton, quaffing a Scotch in the Star: "Anyone would think I'd had a nasty cold. In fact I've just had a lung removed."

He possessed severe good looks eroded by illness and had just inherited the family title. So it was Sir Bruce Seton of Abercorn to whom I was now talking. He talked with breezy optimism about the future but I suspected that this was pure theatre.

Back at the office I called for the cuttings and consulted his ancestry. (*Debrett, Who's Who* and gazetteers are forever to hand on the reporters' and subs' desks.) There in the cuttings, enveloped, annotated and filed, was the life and times of Bruce Seton. From a photograph of a young man with polished hair and Sandhurst-looks to bankruptcy. The transience of mortality encapsulated.

Another event when I met actors off stage and screen was the annual meeting of Equity. They conducted their union business with intelligence, common-sense and elan, but it was nevertheless unsettling to observe them in their grey suits and suede shoes on the platform.

Michael Denison. Shouldn't he have been in court cross-examining some shifty witness trying hopelessly to out-smart him? Marius Goring. Shouldn't he have been wearing the uniform of some swaggering German officer? Richard Attenborough. Playing truant from The Guinea Pig? Robert Flemyng. Looking every inch a headmaster. Shouldn't he have been pulling Richard Attenborough off the stage by his ear?

The only theatrical touch on the platform were the smoked glasses worn by Maurice Kaufman.

XIX

On April 4th., 1957, it was announced that, as from 1960, there would be no further call-ups for National Servicemen.

The announcement coincided with a routine Service story — a complaint from a group of airmen about injustice at their camp. Every day the *Mirror* postbag was weighted with such grievances; many were deflated with one phone call, a few merited a personal visit from a reporter.

Such assignments were always popular. Most of the male reporters had been in the Services either during the war or as post-war National Servicemen and the opportunity to cock a snook at uniformed authority was titillating.

I embarked on these quests with unrestrained enthusiasm. Behind me was a long list of indignities — white-washing coal, scrubbing disgusting frying-pans in the mess tin-room, polishing a corporal's boots in which his socks had mysteriously remained. . . .

I also recalled the unpleasantness at R.A.F. Chivenor in North Devon when, as duty medical orderly, I had to treat a squadron-leader who had been kicked in the private parts while playing rugby. The situation was delicate. Aircraftmen second class were not normally required to handle an officer's testicles. Happily it materialised that he had no wish to have them handled.

"Just give me something to perk me up, laddie," he groaned and collapsed on a couch, one hand inside his baggy blue shorts.

How did you revive an officer hovering painfully on the

borders of impotence? I surveyed the array of bottles on the shelves, many of them unopened because no one knew what they were for. There was the old standby, a bottle labelled enigmatically *Mist. Expec. Stim.* And a bottle of foul-tasting, muddy-looking liquid prescribed by the Medical Officer for patients he thought were skiving.

The only other medicaments with which I was familiar were aspirins, castor oil, acriflavine and a purple fluid used for painting rotten feet. I toyed dreamily with the notion of slapping a boiling-hot kaolin poultice on his parts. . . .

"For Christ's sake get on with it laddie," the figure in the striped jersey growled.

Then I had it. Sal. Volatile, the trusty old restorative. But, unnerved by the bizarre situation, I forgot that it had to be diluted. The officer swigged the dose in one gulp. He smacked his lips for a moment, then sprang from the couch with a terrible cry, hand to his throat. It seemed to have worked, I thought. But did he have to do a Laurence Olivier?

He lurched across the room to the sink and bent over it moaning: "You've killed me, laddie. You've done for me."

I regarded him with alarm and consulted the label on the bottle. I probably had done for him! I filled a glass with water and handed it to him because the only answer seemed to be to dilute the stuff inside him. He gulped it down while I watched him apprehensively wondering what was the prescribed penalty for killing a squadron leader.

Gradually his shuddering subsided and some colour returned to his ashen cheeks. He stared at me with a look of distilled hatred. "Did you do that on purpose, laddie?"

"No sir," and hesitantly: "It seems to have done the trick, sir."

This sent him into a paroxysm of fury. "Name and number, laddie."

"Three treble one eight oh five Lambert D."

"Lamberty? That sounds a bloody stupid name."

"No, sir, Lambert D. Derek," I added, extending the hand of friendship.

But he ignored the gesture. "Well, Lambert D," he said, plunging his hand back into his shorts, "you'll be hearing more about this."

I didn't hear directly but I did see a note on the medical officer's desk asking whether he thought I was a suitable case for promotion. Underneath it the M.O. had scrawled *Totally unsuitable.*

This peremptory dismissal of my talents also owed something to an unfortunate incident when I shot a patient.

I and another orderly had been practising firing an air-rifle along the corridor one quiet Sunday morning and by some fluke of trajectory one of the slugs rounded a corner and plunged into the thigh of a black man recovering from influenza.

He thereupon exaggerated the incident out of all proportion. He accused me of racial prejudice, discharged himself from the sick quarters claiming that his life was in jeopardy and reported me to the sick quarters sergeant.

The incident was suppressed — neither the Medical Officer nor the sergeant wanted anyone to know that their headquarters was used as a rifle-range at weekends — but my R.A.F. career was blighted.

All this and more came back to me when I was dispatched to investigate allegations that a commanding officer had deployed airmen to do his gardening.

Exuding self-importance I strode up to the guardroom, a replica of premises where I had endured humiliations years ago. But the first waft of blanco and floor polish momentarily undermined my confidence.

The last time I had been in a guardroom I had been bumpering the linoleum watched by a corporal with a sardonic wit who never spoke without some reference to copulation.

"I want to see the commanding officer," I said, hearing my voice falter and seeing myself propelling the bumper across the cracked, mirror-bright linoleum.

"Yes, sir. Can I have your name please?"

Sir!

I stared at the sergeant incredulously. He smiled at me. *Smiled!* I looked at the immaculately dressed and polished figure with his peaked cap on the desk beside him. His disciplined features looked familiar. Could he be the one-time corporal who, one bitter morning on the parade ground, had brushed cotton wool across my cheeks and put me on fatigues? (The theory was that, if any cotton-wool adhered to your bristles, then you hadn't shaved properly. In fact I had shaved the previous night.)

'Your name, sir.'

I resisted the temptation to snap to attention and bawl: "Three treble one eight oh five Lambert D" and told him my name. I also told him that I was from the *Daily Mirror*. The effect was electrifying. I thought *he* was going to jump up and salute. Such was the power of the *Mirror* in the military mind at that time.

An appointment had been made the previous day; he found my name on a typewritten list and snatched up the telephone. "The man from the *Mirror's* here, sir," he breathed.

Replacing the receiver, he told me: "There's a car coming right away, sir."

A *car*!

The previous evening I had taken the precaution of meeting airmen from the camp in a pub in a nearby village. They had confirmed that some of them had been digging spuds in the Group Captain's garden.

But the car took me to the adjutant instead of the commanding officer. Again that sense of unreality as I was ushered into the adjutant's office; the feeling can only be appreciated by those who have experienced the *Upstairs, Downstairs* attitude between officers and ranks prevalent in those days.

"Ah, Mr. Lambert." The adjutant, a thinning-haired, pouchy-faced man, looked up. "Take a pew." He pushed a packet of Players across the desk. "Care for a cuppa?"

"Thank you very much."

A plump WAAF was dispatched to brew up. I wondered if she had been instructed to spike mine with bromide.

"And what can we do for you?"

He knew perfectly well what he could do for me. I told him that we had received a letter signed by three airmen alleging that their duties included tending the C.O.'s garden.

"Do you mind if I have their names?"

Yes, I said, I did mind. Newspapers never revealed the source of their information, I told him, imagining the fate of the three erks if their names were divulged.

"It is, of course, an offence to communicate with the Press without authority."

"Perhaps. The fact remains that we have these allegations. It is our duty to get the other side of the story so that we can print a just and accurate report." Once again I was becoming power-mad and pompous with it.

The tea arrived. The WAAF sat down at her typewriter, ears tuned into our conversation.

The adjutant peered at me craftily through the steam rising from his tea. "Supposing I were to say, 'No comment'?"

I shrugged. "That's your privilege. In fact it would give us *carte blanche* to print the story."

That shook him to his socks.

I went on: "In fact I have signed statements that the allegations are true." The lie hovered between us and I drank some tea. "And, as you know, the arrangement was that I was to see the commanding officer."

"He's very busy at the moment."

"I can wait."

The adjutant slumped back in his swivel chair and regarded me moodily. "Very well, I'll see what I can do," he said picking up the telephone.

Five minutes later I was in the presence of the commanding officer who seemed only too pleased to see me and expressed surprise that the adjutant had claimed that he was busy. Another of life's lessons. Always by-pass underlings who have invested themselves with unwarranted authority. Go to the top.

The Group Captain was a burly, avuncular man with

diamond-bright eyes and a pilot's wings on his chest. And he immediately scored psychologically.

"Were you in the R.A.F.?" he asked.

"I was a National Serviceman," I told him. And now, I thought dismally, the whole ignominious tale was going to come out.

"Mmm. Where were you stationed?"

"Padgate, West Kirby, Tangmere, Chivenor. . . ."

"Not overseas?"

"I put in for an overseas posting," I told him, "but that seemed to ensure that I stayed in England."

He grinned. "I know what you mean."

The interview was getting out of hand. I liked the man and that is a disadvantage in investigative journalism.

He said: "So you want to hear about this gardening business. Marvellous, isn't it?"

The familiar feeling that a good story was about to evaporate assailed me.

"Marvellous?" He seemed quite unaware of the enormity of his crime.

"Quite, marvellous. It's the first time I've had genuine volunteers. You know, none of this, 'You, you and you' malarkey."

"You mean they offered their services?"

"Absolutely." He frowned. "Didn't you know that?"

"It wasn't the impression they gave me," I said.

"Ah well, you ask them again. They're mostly country lads. They let it be known that they'd love to do a bit of week-end gardening. They get paid of course. . . ."

That evening I met the part-time gardeners in the pub. Was it true that they had volunteered?

Oh yes, they said blithely, they had volunteered. Hadn't they made that clear?

Driving back to London I reflected that, although I had truculently enjoyed a few moments of glory, the Military had somehow contrived to put 3111805 Lambert D. firmly back in his place.

XX

The next big break after Suez occurred in the summer of 1957 when I was covering a court case in Lewes, Sussex.

I telephoned the office before returning to London to see if there were any queries about my copy. There weren't; instead I was told to stay where I was and ring back in half an hour.

I retired puzzled to a café and waited.

When I called back thirty minutes later I was told to drive to Brighton and call from there. No reason was given.

The crisp orders had a clandestine ring about them. I drove to Brighton and parked my car on the sea-front. It was a chilly, rain-spattered evening and the holidaymakers on the promenade looked grimly defiant in their plastic macs. I went into the foyer of the Metropole, an old hotel with an air of Imperial Russia or Old Vienna about it, and phoned the office.

A high-powered team of Scotland Yard detectives, I was told, were on their way to Brighton to investigate allegations of bribery and corruption within the local police force. A rubber-heel job as it was known.

I asked if the tip was exclusive but the man on the desk didn't know. But it was a magnificent opportunity, he informed me. I didn't need telling: any swipe at authority is always good copy: police investigating police is matchless.

I went into the bar, ordered a drink and considered the position. Where would the men from the Yard stay? Certainly not at the Metropole, the Grand, the Ship, the Royal Albion or any of the other plush watering holes.

I made a hesitant telephone call to Alan Robson, one of the

smartest free-lances in the business, rehearsing some sort of opening pleasantry that wouldn't reveal the true reason for my visit to Brighton.

"Hallo, mate," he said. "You down on the Yard job?"

Alan, a snappily-dressed, fast-talking operator who knew every crook and copper in town showed me where the Yard men were staying. With the help of the facts that he had gathered and my instant local colour I was able to compose an early story.

The Yard team was headed by Commander George Hatherill, deputy chief of the C.I.D. But the policeman responsible for the field work was Detective Superintendent Ian Forbes-Leith, an immaculate, dark-suited figure who looked as though he was a young, up-and-coming financier in the City. Also in the team was Detective Inspector Tommy Butler who was subsequently to devote the last years of his life to nailing the Great Train Robbers.

With the arrival of the London detectives there began a sequence of events that was to extend over many months, daily project Brighton into the headlines and affect the lives of hundreds of people. Not the least of them me.

*   *   *

From the first day the sea-side shell of Brighton was prised open.

Behind the front, where the sea hissed on brown shingle and girls with kiss-me-quick hats brandished candy-floss and men in braces dozed open-mouthed in deckchairs, I found the other Brighton.

I visited seedy clubs, belching pubs, bookmakers' offices, dodgy hotels for naughty weekenders and haunts for homosexuals. I interviewed policemen, pimps, private eyes, fences, bookie's runners, showgirls, pugilists, gangsters and abortionists.

And it was always with surprise that I re-emerged among the Regency terraces, watered lawns and smart restaurants;

173

smelled the salt breezes and watched the sun-burned holiday-makers trooping back to their guest houses.

I don't know of any other town that so deftly embraces Cockney vitality, airs of grace and favour and glimpses of dishonest endeavour. Dirty postcards, embossed visiting cards and betting slips shuffled dexterously together.

Whenever I could I strolled down the Lanes where history was potted and polished in cramped antique shops, or promenaded along one of the two piers which were themselves antiques; as the sea rose and fell among the rusting supports I imagined I could hear marches and waltzes and see mashers with straw boaters and mutton-chop whiskers pursuing bonnetted girls with long trailing skirts. . . .

I fed the hungry slot machines, saw what the lecherous butler had seen thirty years ago, played the football games with headless goal-keepers and forwards with time-chipped knees, drank Guinness in the bar and watched the anglers tucking into their sardine sandwiches, happy to make at least some contact with fish.

In the bars of small hotels I discovered a Society that was Brighton's very own. Middle-aged and elderly couples sitting at tables adorned with carnations and gypsophila taking the waters with their whisky and gin. The men wore blazers and suede shoes, ran second-hand Jaguars, marked the winners in the racing editions of the evening papers and cracked risqué jokes; the women had rouged cheeks and lacquered hair, they wore fur stoles and two-piece costumes which creaked when they moved and they flirted like young girls in Sunday-evening cafés. They were triumphantly enjoying their retirement and they had picked the right spot for it.

Every Friday evening I bade farewell to the fairgrounds, boating pools and fish-and-chip queues and motored home to Mitcham. Every Sunday afternoon I returned. For three months Brighton was my home, Mitcham my weekend resort.

*   *   *

The story was a curious one to cover.

At the best of times policemen only grudgingly handed out information: when they were investigating their own kind they were neurotically reticent. I suffered from the disadvantage that I wasn't a familiar face: the detectives were innately suspicious of strangers and preferred to deal with the crime specialists they knew.

I would call at a pub that I believed was being used as their lunch-time headquarters only to find that they had moved on. Alan Robson, thank God, always seemed to know where they had gone. Better still he and his white-haired father had contacts in the Brighton underworld that compensated for lack of rapport with the London sleuths.

Brighton was by this time in a furore. Crooks who still had something to hide were leaving in droves; others who wanted to settle old scores with the local police were volunteering their services like punters trying to place bets just before the off.

Inside Brighton police station, besieged daily by photographers, the atmosphere was tense. Who was under investigation? And to what did the allegations of bribery and corruption refer? For once the police were discovering what it was like to be the subjects of suspicion.

Jokes about them proliferated in the bars. They were losing their authority. Regrettably the honest cops were suffering alongside those who had precipitated the inquiry — whoever they were.

For the police, both those investigating and those under investigation, it was a traumatic period: for me it was a fascinating three-month excursion into sin. A liberally-cut slice of seed cake.

One late afternoon after I had telephoned my story I was disturbed from the dreamy contemplation of what I considered to be a good tale by an imperious rapping on the door of my hotel bedroom. I opened the door and in walked a devastating creature with long blonde hair, mink stole and ankle-strapped shoes. Unasked, she sat herself in a chair by the

175

window and announced that she had some sensational dis-
closures to make about the police probe.

I examined her dubiously. There were a lot of phoney
stories flying about, a lot of villains trying to slander the
demoralised police force. I was tempted to ask why she hadn't
gone straight to the Scotland Yard team; but if I did she might
stalk out and I might lose an exclusive. Worse, she might give
it to the *Express* or *Mail*.

"Well," I said encouragingly, "what's it all about?"

"How about buying a girl a drink," she said, drawing up her
skirt and exposing a generous length of leg.

The age of chivalry wasn't yet dead even if, as I suspected,
my visitor was a sea-front tart. "What would you like?"

"That's very kind of you I'm sure. My usual tipple is
whisky. A large one if you can run to it."

I poured two whiskies from the bottle of Johnny Walker I
had brought to the room to circumnavigate Room Service
charges and added water from the wash-basin tap.

"Here's looking at you," she said, direct from *Casablanca*,
except that she was no Ingrid Bergman and I was certainly no
Humphrey Bogart. "You live well you boys, don't you."

"Fair to middling," I said.

"I wanted to be a writer once." She tossed her golden mane
and smiled sadly. She was devastating enough in a used sort of
way and yet. . . .

"Didn't we all," I said.

"But you *do* write, dearie. It must be wonderful to be
creative. I've read all your pieces in the *Mirror*."

Flattery will get you everywhere. I warmed to her and
smiled. "Another whisky?"

"Don't mind if I do. Easy on the water."

"Well," I said as she snatched the glass from my hand,
"what have you got to tell me?"

"You'd be surprised."

"I bet I would," wondering if a fiver would do the trick.

"They had it coming to them, didn't they?"

"Who had it coming to them?"

176

"The law, that's who."

Stuffily I said: "Whatever comes out I still think we've got the best police force in the world. There are always one or two rogues. . . ."

"I suppose you're right. I'm not one to harbour malice."

Here comes the revelation, I thought. Instead she said: "Do you find me attractive?"

Suddenly I had a vision of her tearing off her clothes and yelling: "Rape."

"No doubt about it," I said soothingly.

"A lot of men do."

"I'm sure they do."

This seemed to satisfy her for the moment. She sipped her whisky reflectively and stared out of the window while I steeled myself to hear the life story of a golden-hearted tom.

Gently I said: "Now about this information you've got." I took a crumpled fiver from my wallet and laid it on the bed-side table.

The effect was startling. She stared at the note for a moment as though it were a cockroach that had crawled out of the woodwork, then stood up dramatically and said: "You just don't care, do you?"

"I beg your pardon?"

"You don't care about my feelings."

"I'm sorry. . . ."

"You knew all along, didn't you?"

"Knew what?"

She tore the wig from her head and showed me what: a crew-cut.

Wig in hand, she strode from the room. I never discovered what it was she had come to expose. But I had a shrewd suspicion.

A couple of days later I interviewed a pick-pocket in a pub frequented by the racing fraternity. He claimed he had given information to the visiting policemen but was as reluctant as my transvestite visitor to go into details.

He was a mournful little man with thin, fluttering hands

177

that darted around his pockets. Perhaps in lean times he robbed himself.

The tables in the lounge, a spartan place with a few prints of impossibly-muscled racehorses on the walls, were littered with copies of *Sporting Life*. At the bar stood a few well-nourished bookies and under-nourished ex-jockeys.

My informant was a compulsive criminal. He had spent much of his life in prison and referred to various jails like a seasoned traveller mulling over his favourite resorts. Inside or outside, it was all the same to him. He boasted that he had once removed the keys from a jailer without him knowing and attributed his downfall to lifting a wallet from a detective at Brighton racecourse.

He was, he confided, due for a stretch inside. Winter was approaching and his thin fingers lost their agility in the cold weather. He would wait until he knew he was under observation and then clumsily try and pinch a gold-watch from some toff.

"You'd be surprised how easy the mugs make it for us," he told me. "Sometimes if I see a wallet sticking out of the back pocket of a geezer's trousers I don't even try to nick it. It's an insult to our trade." He preferred, he said, to rob a toff who had taken the trouble to have an inside pocket inserted in the left side of his jacket. "They seem to think we always prefer to dip the right-hand side and it narks them when we rumble them."

He had always worked alone, spurning the aid of an accomplice to create a diversion. "But if you get bumped in a crowd grab the geezer on the other side. Not that you stand much chance. Always best to leave your lolly at home."

"But why did you go to the police?" I asked.

He looked aggrieved. "I didn't. They came to me. They always do. I don't know why, I've never snitched in my life. I reckon they just like a nice chat."

There didn't seem much point in pursuing the conversation. I bought him another drink and prepared to depart.

"Just one thing before you do," he said, hands fluttering like butterflies.

"What's that?"

"You'd better have your wallet back," he said, handing it to me.

In a basement flat of one of the elegant Regency houses from which well-heeled residents surveyed the town through windows doing service as monocles I interviewed a con-man who lectured me on the extraordinary gullibility of his victims.

With his clipped white moustache he looked like a retired Indian Army colonel. An unlikely con-man; but then, of course, they all are. His barely credible speciality was a ploy with cement balls.

He and an accomplice would select a mug, often a small-time shop-keeper. Then, dramatically changing his appearance, the colonel would become a White Russian count who had fled from the Bolsheviks, bringing with him an enormous quantity of cement balls in which he had hidden priceless gold coins. But he had fallen on hard times. . . . Gabbling away in some language invented on the spot he would produce a gold coin.

Another customer— an accomplice— who just happened to speak Russian told the shop-keeper that the coin was a sample from a cement ball.

"You expect me to believe that?"

The customer translated the shopkeeper's remark. Another torrent of gibberish. The customer informed the shop-keeper: "He says he doesn't care whether you believe him or not. But he has got another cement ball on his person. Have you got a hammer?"

The shop-keeper would produce a hammer. A concrete ball would be placed on the counter. Crack! And another golden yolk would roll out.

More gibberish.

Helpful customer: "He says you called him a liar. He wants an apology."

"But. . . ."

Contemptuously the count would pick up the coin, replace it with its fellow in his pocket, and stalk out of the shop.

The customer would then whisper: "Are you interested?" and, when the bemused shop-keeper indicated that he might be, he would rush after the count.

They would return a couple of days later where once more the count would crack open another cement ball — "For the sake of my honour" — and sweep imperiously from the shop.

On their last visit the shop-keeper would agree to buy several thousand cement balls for as much as £1,500. The helpful customer would take the money and count it while the count cracked one more ball on the counter.

The count then indulged himself in a last speech which the customer translated as: "The Count says that, as he is a man of honour, he wants you to hold the money while he goes and fetches the rest of the balls."

They both then departed leaving the shop-keeper holding a wad of notes that the customer had substitued for the real money while he was watching the cracking of the last cement ball. The wad consisted of a £5 note at the top and the bottom and a considerable amount of plain paper in between.

I told the colonel that it sounded an incredibly elaborate way to con someone out of £1,500.

"Maybe, old boy," he said, "but it works. It's so fantastic that it never occurs to anyone that we're pulling anything as mundane as a switch."

"But they must discover almost immediately that they've been conned."

"They do, old boy. But by that time we've scarpered. And they don't go to the police because they look so damned ridiculous. Those are our strengths — the mugs' reluctance to appear stupid and their greed."

"Don't any of them go to the police?" I asked, reflecting that the colonel had just come out of prison.

"One or two," he admitted regretfully. "One or two of the bounders do."

On a park-bench I met by appointment a man who had been described to me as a hit-man.

He wore a tan leather coat, dark glasses and expensive brown shoes. He was young with soft black hair and expressionless white features.

"How much is it worth?" he asked in a voice that was almost a whisper. Behind the dark glasses his eyes appraised me.

"Depends what you've got to offer."

"Fifty pounds for some of the contracts I've carried out?"

"I'd have to consult the office."

"They were big ones," he murmured. "Really big ones." He spoke like a man reluctantly and prematurely in retirement.

"I'd have to name you in the paper."

"It doesn't matter. You see there's a contract out for me."

The park was lit with pale sunshine and chrysanthemum blooms touched by frost hung like crunched-up coloured handkerchieves. Across the exhausted grass a boy threw sticks for his dog.

Beside me death.

"Can we meet here tomorrow?" I asked.

"As you wish. But don't leave it too long."

I stood up. "Very well. Same time tomorrow."

He didn't get up. I wondered what colour his eyes were behind the dark glasses. But I didn't immediately telephone the office because I was becoming canny; instead I consulted a friendly Brighton detective.

"What did he look like?" the detective asked.

I described the man in the park.

"That's Ralph," the detective told me.

"Is he a killer?"

"He's a killer all right — on the stage. He's an out-of-work actor. Brighton's full of them."

I didn't return to the park. But I often wondered if Ralph had reached a point in his ailing theatrical career where he had decided to live the parts he played.

181

During the ensuing weeks the long arm of the law stretched like a contortionist's back through the years; and skeletons rattled in cupboards as stocky men wearing brown or grey hats and square-shouldered overcoats were admitted into homes where it had been believed that all had been forgiven and forgotten.

Hundreds of statements were taken; the detectives travelled all over Britain following up leads. In Brighton no one could consider themselves outside the remorseless curiosity of the Scotland Yard officers who hated what they were doing but were determined to do it.

I met an abortionist, a placid housewife with crimped grey hair, who genuinely believed that she was carrying out a social service; a street photographer who never put a film in his camera; a fence who boasted that he wouldn't pay more than £500 for the Crown Jewels; a cat-burglar with a broken leg; a rheumy-eyed alcoholic who drank a bottle of Scotch before lunch.

Wintry winds blew away summer; the holidaymakers departed and their deck-chairs were folded up and put into hibernation; and still there didn't appear to be an end in sight to the investigation.

After the first hectic weeks the crime specialists only put in guest appearances. The arrival of these heavies sharpened the wits of those of us who had taken up residence because it always heralded "a dramatic development". We dropped our newspapers, gulped our coffee, pocketed our notebooks and bowled along the sea-front to Dr. Brighton's, the famous old pub where news was gathered, collated and, if deadlines were approaching, dispatched.

Thanks to Robson the story was working out well for me. Arrests pending, mystery witnesses, dramatic dashes. . . . A couple of exclusives and a host of page leads appeared under my byline. Surely the climax to the story had to come soon.

But the Yard determined to take its time, to *proceed* on its investigation.

During lulls in developments we enjoyed the raffish charms

182

of out-of-season Brighton. Competed with Winchester repeating rifles on the end of one of the piers; visited the music-hall; toured the Royal Pavilion; mingled with the young bloods and spirited girls attending the annual conference of the Young Conservatives. Some of the girls seemed to find the company of the Press fascinating, and romance — or something like it— briefly blossomed between nubile young Tories and bachelor newspapermen.

I became friendly with a blonde with a Bridgette Bardot figure who endlessly interrogated me about my political affiliations in the lounge of the Metropole.

"But how *can* you work for the *Mirror*," she would ask, thirstily drinking a gin-and-tonic. "I mean you're not a Socialist, or anything like that, are you?"

"I'm not anything. I don't have any strong political views."

"But that's terrible. You must have a social conscience. It's only apathy that lets *them* seize power."

Privately I thought that her intensity adequately compensated for the apathy of half a dozen like me.

On the third gin-and-tonic she would thrust out her magnificent bosom and lecture me sternly on the advantages of capitalism and free enterprise.

"I'm not a Tory and I'm not a Socialist," I would say. "I'm your actual floating voter and if I ever stood for Parliament I would be an independent." I felt like a humble native in the presence of a zealous missionary.

"But that's just spineless."

I hung my head in shame.

She spoke volubly and articulately and would doubtless convert flocks of dissenters in the future. But not me: I valued my ambivalent attitude too highly. I have since forgotten her name. Perhaps it was Margaret.

By mid-October the story was beginning to pall and badly needed a shot in the arm. On October 8th it got it: a Brighton detective was arrested and at 12.18 p.m. stood in the dock charged with attempting to obtain a sum of money "as a reward for showing favour in affairs relating to the Crown."

*   *   *

More arrests and court appearances followed and finally we embarked on reporting the committal proceedings. A committal was always a tedious affair because question and answer had to be laboriously recorded; it also took the bite out of the subsequent trial much of which was repetition. Today, unless a defendant asks for reporting restrictions to be lifted, revelations in newspapers of lower court hearings are drastically curbed.

One of the tricks to avoid transcribing and dictating column after column of evidence was to persuade your office to allow you to write a couple of pages covering the salient points garnished with background colour material. If you were sufficiently persuasive then you could close with an instruction to the sub-editor to take in agency copy.

I succeeded in this manoeuvre because, with our early editions, it was to the sub-editor's advantage to deal with the reams of agency copy as early as possible. Then he had only to slap my intro on top of it.

So the extended sojourn beside the sea continued into the winter. The defendants were duly committed for trial and I took up the story again in February, 1958, when they appeared at the Old Bailey.

Five men were accused of conspiring together and with other persons unknown to obstruct the course of public justice between January 1st, 1949 and October 18th, 1957. One of them was the Chief Constable. Of the other four one was a detective inspector, one a sergeant and two were civilians — a licensee and a bookmaker.

The array of barristers — including a stunning girl with heart-rending legs named Ann Curnow who has since prospered in her profession — was impressive, the atmosphere taut. And even if the evidence was rather less than sensational — mostly allegations of favours and bribes — the story held the headlines for nineteen days.

In the Old Bailey canteen and the Magpie and Stump across

the street it was like a reunion for us journalists. One by one we saw our Brighton contacts follow one another into the witness box. The tension reached a crescendo with a five and a half hour adjournment by the jury.

Finally the Chief Constable and the licensee were acquitted. The detective inspector, the sergeant and the bookmaker were gaoled. When my full background story appeared I swaggered around the office as though I were carrying a banner around with my byline on it. Deciding that enough was enough, Ken Hord dispatched me to a doorstep. It was as though I had just returned from a day trip to the seaside.

XXI

It was around 1958 that I first began to feel that, on the *Mirror*, my horizons were limited. The *Mirror* was in no way to blame: it believed rightly that its strength lay in its domestic coverage. Nevertheless as the Russians launched their first satellite, as the Treaty of Rome was signed, as the Mau Mau atrocities gathered momentum in Kenya, I lapsed occasionally into restlessness.

At this stage in the beatnik and bobby-sox era this was not too disquieting because there were home-side stories of the moment to cover — Eden's resignation, Macmillan's appointment as Prime Minister, Notting Hill race riots, the first Premium Bond draw. . . .

And I still managed zestfully to enjoy the bizarre and humorous aspects of life to which *Mirror* reporting introduced me. Many of these originated in the waiting room. But there the danger was the cranks because it wasn't always easy to distinguish them among the host of visitors who daily called upon their favourite newspaper with genuine information and grievances.

But we did get to know our regulars. The tiny waiting room was just outside the sliding doors beside the reporters' desks. When a messenger brought up a visitor it was sometimes just possible to catch a glimpse of him.

If he or she was a regular there was a mass exodus to the toilet. But that didn't phase the astute newsdesk man. He merely stood outside the locked door of a closet and said:

"Derek, when you're finished, there's someone in the waiting room for you."

All you could do then was get it over and done with.

Of the cranks the most common were those with a persecution complex. The police were persecuting them, the Inland Revenue, the local council. . . .

Many criminals released from jail that morning also gravitated to the *Mirror* like homing pigeons with horrendous descriptions of conditions inside H.M. Prisons. Perhaps they were true but there wasn't much we could do about them.

Occasionally a dangerous nutter put in an appearance. One such visitor rejected the civilities of the waiting room and was seen roaming around the various floors of the building holding, according to witnesses, a gun. A burly printer finally cornered him in the canteen and he was brought down in a rugby tackle in a welter of fish and chips and mugs of tea. No gun was found and he was ejected.

One popular journalistic strategem as a client began to undo the string round a brown-paper parcel containing documented evidence of some extraordinary phenomenon was to dispatch him forthwith to a rival newspaper.

"Just a minute, sir. You did say Martians?"

"That's right. They landed in my garden again this morning. Little green fellows."

"Ah. Then I've good news for you."

"Walking all over my lettuces they were."

"And the good news is that Martians are right up the *Daily Sketch's* street."

"But. . . ."

"I'll give them a call while you're on your way," manhandling him out of the door.

The crunch came when he broke free and said: "But the *Sketch* sent me round to you."

The most difficult customers to handle were the border-line cases with information that might or might not make a story. You then faced the alarming prospect of being lost in a jungle

187

of conflicting facts while a story broke in Bermuda or the South of France.

Informants on the telephone could also be a tease. They were first put through to the newsdesk and then deftly passed onto a reporter. Some of the calls were enigmatic in the extreme.

"Meet me under the clock at Waterloo Station in half an hour and you'll learn something to your advantage."

"Thank you Mr. . . ."

"Never mind about my name, matey. You just get yourself down here."

"But. . . ."

"No bleeding if's or but's. Do you want a good story or don't you?"

"But how will I recognise you?"

"You won't," ominously, "I'll recognise you."

Fear of missing a story is ever uppermost in a newspaperman's mind so, unless all hell was breaking loose elsewhere, we kept the appointment.

The results of these sinister summonses were varied.

Anything from the discovery of a mass grave beneath the floorboards of a suburban house to a mystery allergy affecting a pet rabbit.

Crime reporters had dozens of informants: I had one. A Mr. Cash. Cash almost certainly wasn't his name, more a reminder that he expected to be recompensed for his tips. He was a policeman but, sadly, not of very high rank. Thus his tips tended to be mundane. Nevertheless they could not be ignored.

I never knew his true identity. He was, I suspected, a detective I had met on a story. But I was very fond of him: he was *my informant*.

He seemed to be allotted an inordinate amount of night duties because the telephone would usually ring beside my bed in the early hours of the morning. Rousing myself from the depths of sleep I would pick up the phone hopefully expecting to hear Mike Anderson, the night news editor, telling me to stand by at London Airport with my passport.

Instead I heard: "Cash here."

"Good morning Mr. Cash, what have you got?"

The trouble with Mr. Cash was that he spoke in the strange language affected by policemen, criminals and crime reporters. Half-asleep, it was difficult to translate messages interspersed with suss, drum and nick.

"Come again Mr. Cash?"

With a sigh he would repeat the riddle while I made notes on the pad beside my bed. When I had finally solved it I would call the office and impart the information.

"Where does it come from, old man?"

"One of my informants," hoping that I had given the impression that an army of underworld contacts was ceaselessly at work on my behalf.

At first I hoped that if I paid Mr. Cash by cheque, I might get some clue to his identity when the cheque was returned with my bank statement. But Mr. Cash was having none of that. All payments — ten bob usually — had to be sent by post to a box number.

In cash.

*   *   *

Animals still occupied a large part of my time. Horses, dogs, monkeys, bunnies, hampsters, inhabitants of the London Zoo and the very occasional cat. Betty Tay dealt with the big animal stories. Horses rescued from the knacker's yard, dogs that had saved children from fires, VIP animals mating in the Zoo and the cubs or whatever that resulted.

General news reporters followed up lesser animal stories but, with careful handling, these often developed into passable tales. But it was with considerable misgivings that, in the company of Tommy Lea, I set out for a North London suburb to listen to a singing dog.

189

Talking dogs had already been covered by Noel Whitcomb in his column. A canine vocal act was something new. What would it be, basso profundo or tenor? Soprano or contralto? Perhaps a touch of the Sinatra's.

We stopped outside an end-terrace in a street of small Victorian houses that seemed to have more than the usual allocation of dogs, a whole pack of them racing along the pavements watched aloofly by slit-eyed cats taking the sun on window-ledges. Perhaps our dog was giving a concert.

The door of No. 12 was opened by a middle-aged man wearing the trousers and waistcoat of a blue suit, a shirt with a gold stud but no collar or tie, and a peaked cap. He was, presumably, Mr. Kedge, the dog's owner.

We told him we were from the *Mirror* and he said: "I suppose you've come about our Percy. You're in luck, he's in good voice today."

We walked into a neat parlour where, despite the warm day, a small coal-fire burned in the grate. On the hob stood a blackened kettle, steam issuing from its spout.

Mrs. Kedge, a plump woman with her hair in curlers, came in from the kitchen carrying a tray loaded with chinking cups. "I expect you'd like a nice cup of tea," she said.

We sipped the scalding brew feeling as though we were indulging in pre-curtain drinks. It was a cosy scene and only one participant was missing — our Percy.

At that moment what I had taken to be a hearth-rug moved slightly and Mrs. Kedge said: "I do believe Percy is waking up."

We stared at the apparition laboriously getting to its feet in front of the fire. It was long and brown with a tail like a palm frond and a gentle, spaniel face framed with floppy ears. It was, for a dog, immensely tall.

Percy surveyed us for a moment while we waited breathlessly, swished his tail a couple of times and then, overcome by the effort, collapsed again in front of the fire and went to sleep.

"Never hits a note unless our Len's here," Mr. Kedge said.

"Len?"

190

"Yes, our Len. He'll be down in a minute. Sleeps late of a morning does our Len."

This was manifestly true because it was 1.30 p.m.

Apologetically Tommy asked who Len might be.

"Our lad," Mrs. Kedge said. Her accent came from somewhere between the Midlands and the North Country. "He trained our Percy."

"What does Percy sing?" I asked, acutely aware of the lunatic quality of the conversation.

"You name it," Mr. Kedge said promptly and, I thought, a little defensively.

"Another cup of tea?" asked Mrs. Kedge.

"No thanks. Do you think Len will be down soon?"

"Takes his time does Len."

The attitude of the Kedges to their son seemed to be so servile that I had by this time formed a vision of some hulking unshaven tyrant in hob-nailed boots.

In a cage in the corner two blue budgerigars twittered to each other. For the want of something better to say Tommy asked if they talked. The Kedges looked at Tommy as though he were mad. The very idea of budgerigars talking!

Upstairs we heard the creak of floorboards. Our Len was about to make his entrance. All eyes were trained on the stairs as a thin, pale youth with Mickey Mouse ears and water-slicked hair appeared yawning cavernously.

Percy opened one eye, yawned and let his eyelid fall again like a camera shutter. I began to wonder if sleepy sickness was endemic in the house.

"The *Mirror's* here, Len," Mrs. Kedge said.

Len regarded us without enthusiasm and said: "Is dinner ready yet, mum?" He was wearing striped pyjamas and a moulting dressing-gown.

"All in good time," Mr. Kedge said with the faintest trace of authority. "First we want a few songs."

"Blimey not again," Len said coming down the stairs. He had been brought up in London because his whining voice was edged with Cockney vowels.

191

"What do you mean not again?" I asked, wondering if Percy had sung for other papers.

Mrs. Kedge explained: "Len had some of his friends round last night. Percy sang a couple of numbers for them."

The doormat trembled faintly at the mention of his name.

Len looked us up and down contemptuously and said: "What's it worth?"

A good kick up the rump, I thought. "We'll talk about that after Percy's sung," I said. "Now, does he sing or doesn't he?"

"'Course he does," Len said. "'Course you sing, don't you, Percy." No movement from the body in front of the fire.

Mrs. Kedge said in a coaxing voice: "Get your mouth-organ out, Len."

Grumbling and scratching Len produced a mouth-organ from a drawer in the sideboard. He ejected a small deposit of spittle and blew a few chords of what vaguely sounded like *Onward Christian Soldiers*.

The dog whimpered in its sleep.

"Come on Percy," Mr. Kedge implored.

"Just leave him to me, dad," Len said. "It's not you that's going on the halls with him."

Mrs. Kedge said: "I expect he'll be on telly after he's been in the *Mirror*. Do you want to take a picture, Mr. Photographer?"

Tommy apologised and said he'd leave it until after the recital.

"Well," I said irritably, "let's get on with it."

"Don't rush it," Len said staring coldly at me. "He's got to be in the mood."

"Well get him in the mood."

Len held up one hand. "All in my own good time."

He blew a piercing note on the mouth-organ. "On your feet, Percy. Sing for the *Mirror*."

Once again the dog dragged itself to its feet and stood, tongue hanging out, blinking sleepily at Len.

"*Onward Christian Soldiers*, Percy. Okay?"

Percy yawned.

"Right, here we go."

192

I wasn't musical and it had always seemed to me that the first five notes or so of *Onward Christian Soldiers* were much the same as each other.

Len blew the first note and waited. After a moment or two Percy let out a mournful howl.

"That's fine, Percy," Len said. "That's great. Keep at it boy."

He blew another note and Percy emitted another heart-rending bellow. Len gave me one of those looks that are supposed to silence cynics. Another blast on the mouth-organ, another agonising noise from Percy. This was followed by a sound like a piano string being plucked from somewhere inside Percy.

Len looked accusingly at Mrs. Kedge. "Has he been fed, mum?"

Mrs. Kedge wrung her hands. "You know he eats with us."

"How do you expect him to sing on an empty stomach?"

"Len," I said, "I'm a patient man. But could you kindly get on with it?"

The *Christian Soldiers* proceeded onwardly at a funereal pace for another couple of notes to the point where, if my limited musical appreciation was correct, Percy would have to change his tune.

Len played a different note: Percy opened his slavering chops but no noise emerged.

Mr. Kedge nudged me. "He doesn't always get that one," he confided.

"But I thought you said he sang. You know, actually *sang*."

"What do you think he's doing then?" Mr. Kedge asked indignantly.

Len played another note identical to the first five and Percy responded as before, then collapsed to the floor overcome by the effort.

Even Len seemed to be aware that today Percy wasn't another Richard Tauber. "Of course," he said, "we've got a bit more rehearsing to do yet."

Not wanting to upset Mr. and Mrs. Kedge I said: "I think you're right. He's not quite ready for the big-time yet."

As Tommy picked up his camera bag I took Len by the arm and led him towards the front door. "You know something, lad?"

"What's that?" Len asked sulkily.

"Why don't you take up speech-training and get cracking with those budgies?"

We emerged into the sunlight where the pack of dogs, unfettered by operatic aspirations, was still bounding joyously up and down the street.

*   *   *

Publicity stunts, facility trips, hoaxes, tales of the supernatural . . . all such propositions had to be approached with extreme caution.

The essence of a good publicity stunt is to circumnavigate editors' aversion to the inclusion of advertising material in the editorial columns. Advertisements, the editors rightly maintain, should be paid for.

The stunt, then, must be newsworthy in its own right and it must be sufficiently plausible to assuage journalistic conscience. It is no good flying an aircraft emblazoned with the name of some brand product under Tower Bridge; it is futile to employ an athlete to cycle backwards to Land's End proclaiming at every halt that he attributes his powers of endurance to a new patent elixir.

The publicist must also accept the fact that an extravagant stunt can disintegrate into a financially disastrous failure.

One entrepreneur telephoned the picture desk of a national newspaper and suggested that it would considerably enhance the paper's reputation for enterprise if he arranged for seventy-six trombonists — a reference to a song from the show *The Music Man* — to parade at dawn outside Brixton Prison. An assistant on the desk, his mind on more noble matters, absent-mindedly agreed that it would be, if nothing else, an unusual photograph.

The following morning dawned with a bitter East wind stalking the streets. Pedestrians and motorists on their way to work were treated to the spectacle of seventy-six shivering, blue-nosed trombonists stamping their feet outside the walls of the prison.

From time to time one of them would blow a despairing note while the entrepreneur tried to explain to the suspicious police the purpose of the extraordinary visitation. Finally he called the newspaper and discovered to his chagrin that, not only had the assistant forgotten to pass on his message, but that the picture editor himself wasn't the slightest bit interested. With a few discordant notes of disgust the musicians dispersed in search of more conventional employment.

Facility trips constituted one of the great tests of journalistic discrimination. Patently no organisation was paying for travel, food and accommodation for purely philanthropic reasons.

The motives varied from the need to publicise a new air route to far more sinister endeavours to politically or militarily mislead correspondents. Whatever the correspondent wrote the suspicion always existed that he was corruptly inveigled into doing so. But what if the facility trip was the only means of obtaining information? The only solution was to insist on paying all 'expenses.

Hoaxes rarely made satisfactory stories. They contained none of the natural elements of humour and served principally to satisfy the ego of the half-wits who perpetrated them.

One hoax that I covered, however, was an extraordinary affair and I never understood the motives behind it.

The hoaxer, posing as a sanitary inspector, persuaded the occupants of seventeen houses in Helen Street, Woolwich, that their homes were going to be pulled down. He even accompanied a party of householders to a new estate where, he claimed, they would be rehoused. To keep in his good books they fed and entertained him.

One man scrubbed his home from top to bottom to try and persuade the *inspector* that there was no need for him to move;

195

another woman stood back while the *inspector* carried out what he described as a smoke test on her drains.

But there wasn't a whiff of smoke. The woman called the police and the hoaxer was exposed. He was only seventeen; but I never found him and never discovered what strange Freudian impulse set him to work.

Tales of the supernatural were also suspect — the supernatural usually turning out to be natural — and most of the ghosts wandered the streets directly after closing-time. Not that I ever rejected out of hand any forces operating outside the bounds of nature. To neither believe nor disbelieve seemed to be the only reasonable attitude to adopt.

Some close friends of mine claimed that their furniture was regularly re-arranged in their lounge while they were asleep upstairs; perfectly rational acquaintances had at seances received messages based on information that seemingly could not have been known to the medium.

But psychic phenomenon had to be pretty damn convincing to survive the scrutiny of reporter, news-desk assistant, copy-taker and chief-sub, all trained like mechanics tuning an engine, to detect a false note.

I attended a seance held by a man and a woman to try and determine the cause of death of the man's wife. At a previous seance her death from a stomach ailment had been forecast. Eight months later she had died in hospital after an operation for appendicitis.

The man who claimed he wasn't satisfied about the circumstances placed the letters of the alphabet written on squares of paper around a circular table. He and the woman friend then placed their forefingers on an upturned wineglass and asked his wife if she could help.

The glass certainly spelled out sentences and a name. But nothing conclusive emerged. And it was impossible to determine whether, unconsciously, the two participants were themselves spelling out the replies.

Inconclusive or not, the story made the front-page lead. It

was, I suppose, the ambivalent nature of the replies that made it all that more plausible.

The arrival of Johann Sebastian Bach in a cottage in rural Kent was less easy to swallow.

I drove to the cottage one Sunday in November to investigate a letter from a couple who claimed that the composer had come to lodge with them. They had seen his ghostly figure ascending the stairs and in the evenings they heard music coming from the attic.

The couple were elderly and homely and apparently sincere in their beliefs. We waited until the evening; then the husband, thin-framed and gentle-faced, switched off the light. The room was lit by flames from a log-fire. Outside, the branches of a tree scratched the window. Then we heard a creak on the stairs.

The wife, a little wisp of a woman with an autumn-leaf face, said: "There he goes."

I opened the door leading into the hall but there was no one there. The husband went up the stairs returning a few minutes later. Almost immediately we heard the faint strains of music.

The husband cocked his head for a moment, then said: "Brandenburg No. 2." He had, it transpired, been a musician.

"I'd better go up and have a look," I said.

"But you'll disturb him," the wife said.

And the entire orchestra which Johann Sebastian had somehow managed to assemble in the attic!

Beneath the entrance to the attic stood a step-ladder. When I was half way up it became apparent that the orchestra was in a rebellious mood because they were repeating one phrase of music.

The ancient gramophone complete with horn stood on struts of wood beside the water-tank. I gently lifted the pick-up arm and replaced it so that Brandenburg No. 2 could continue without further interruption.

"Well?"

They looked at me eagerly, faces alight with anticipation.

"He's there all right," I said. They sighed contentedly and I departed without even attempting to analyse the deception they were playing upon themselves.

It certainly wasn't doing anyone any harm.

XXII

By 1959 my restlessness had become feverish.

I had been on the *Mirror* for six years and u.: ci.ances of advancement were remote. I should like to have been posted to a foreign bureau; but the staffmen in the bureaux — New York, Paris, Rome, Bonn — were firmly entrenched and nothing less than an outbreak of bubonic plague would shift them.

The alternative was a job on the news desk or the subs' table. But I hadn't entered journalism to be chair-bound.

I had to go.

The decision was a distressing one. The *Mirror* was a happy office; what's more its standards of tabloid journalism were the highest in the world.

So it was with a paranoic sense of guilt that I began to make furtive advances to other papers. Not directly, of course, because I didn't want it to get around that I needed a job. In Fleet Street this would be interpreted as: "I hear Lambert got the old heave-ho."

No, I had to make it known that I was available — at a price. I leaked my availability in the Press Club (not too brashly in case the message was picked up by *Mirror* antennae); I materialised in opposition pubs on the rare occasions that I had pulled off an exclusive.

I circulated as industriously as a Salvation Army soldier selling *War Cry*. All to no avail. Whereas other reporters were lured to opposition papers by the promise of extravagant salaries my market value wasn't even quoted.

Temporary relief from the gloom into which my abortive efforts had plunged me came from an unlikely source.

Not Fidel Castro's take-over in Cuba, not the landing of a Russian satellite on the moon, not the Tory's 100 overall majority in the General Election. Nothing like that. Andy Capp was my temporary saviour.

Smythe's cartoons of the indolent, unemployed, beer-swigging layabout with a peaked cap squatting on his nose, had only been appearing in the *Mirror* for a relatively short time. But his elevation to the place he now holds in our social structure alongside *Coronation Street* was already assured.

While interviewing some soldiers with a grievance I discovered that a group of Royal Engineers stationed at Maidstone, Kent, had formed an Andy Capp club. My journalist senses quivered; I telephoned the Army authorities who imparted the joyous information that the unit had been posted to Germany.

I now had to proceed cannily to prevent the story being appropriated by one of the staffmen on the Continent. It was easier than I anticipated: the news desk seemed to think that, if I had any claims at all to specialisation, it was in the direction of indolent, beer-swigging layabouts. I departed for Osnabruck with a talented photographer named Bob Hope who stoically endured endless jokes about Bing Crosby and Dorothy Lamour.

The story turned out to be a *Mirror* natural. Off-duty, the fifteen members of the club all wore flat caps pulled over their eyes; they conversed with cigarettes stuck to their lips; they quaffed steins of lager in the musty beer cellars of Osnabruck.

Membership fee was a pint (or a stein); the fine for breaking club rules was a round of drinks; the aim was to promote the cause of poor, down-trodden *would-be* Andy Capps all over the world. They talked about football, greyhounds, racing pigeons and the Florries — Florrie is Mr. Capp's long-suffering wife — they had left behind.

The Germans were impressed. In an inn called the Green Hunter a white-haired industralist eagerly snatched his feath-

200

ered Tyrolean hat from his head and bawled: "We exchange, ja?"

"We exchange nein," said one of the members. "But you can try on an Andy if you like."

The story was slapped across the centre-page spread with an Andy Capp cartoon in the bottom corners. Sapper Dave Cotton, twenty-one, from Portsmouth, proved to be an archetypal Capp and was pictured with his peaked cap a regulation one inch below his eyes, a NAAFI pint in his fist and a cigarette drooping from his mouth.

I concluded the story with a monstrous pun. *Sapper Brian Boswell, 20, from Barnes, London, missed a club meeting because he was on guard duty.*

"It was a bit of an 'andicap," he told me.

If ever I deserved a spell of late shifts it was then.

*   *   *

Whenever you were abroad one of the priorities was to find another story to keep you there. After the Andy Capp assignment I found some feeble excuse to take me to Hamburg; the story, again about Servicemen, flickered feebly for a couple of hours before I was reluctantly forced to snuff it out as the phoney it transparently was.

But I was still left with a night in Hamburg. I booked into the splendid old Four Seasons Hotel and headed with ungainly speed for the wicked streets around the Reperbahn.

I visited various bars and clubs. In the first stout German women were wrestling in mud; this seemed an unedifying spectacle so I moved on to an establishment where primly-dressed girls could be hired as dancing partners for a few marks. But there weren't as prim as they seemed because the dance-floor was made of mirrors and it soon became apparent that they wore no knickers under their skirts; even a slow waltz degenerated into the Eton Wall game as the men blindly pushed their partners around, eyes firmly fixed on the floor.

201

I adjourned to another club where each table bore a number and was equipped with a telephone. If a man fancied a girl— or a hostess fancied an affluent-looking customer — he or she dialled the number of the appropriate table.

I had been sitting at Table No. 4 quietly sipping an extortionately expensive lager for five minutes or so when my telephone rang. A husky female asked in broken-English if I would like to buy a girl a drink; I gazed across the floor and saw the blonde personification of Teutonic beauty looking at me and speaking into a telephone.

Why not? No harm done.

"I'll buy you a beer," I said, having seen too many customers taken to the dry-cleaners in Soho clip-joints.

I replaced the receiver but, alarmingly, the voice continued. "You know somezing? You is my type. And vot is so comical is zat we need never haf used ze instrument."

I turned and saw, sitting at the table next to me, a woman whom the casting director of Hammer films had somehow missed. She had long, grey-rooted black hair, sunken cheeks and painted bow-lips fashionable in Mary Pickford's day.

"Is zat not a hoot?"

She moved swiftly to my table and sat gazing at me through sunken eyes, one of which had received recent attentions from a fist. Behind us a waiter hovered incredulously. Across the floor the Amazonian blonde was still prattling into her telephone.

I bought my companion a beer because it was the least I could do, excused myself and fled into the night where the crew of a Royal Navy destroyer was limbering up for its own interpretation of a good-will visit to Hamburg.

In another club I was introduced to the star attraction, a girl trapeze artist who confided that her husband was a Chinese wrestler; not wanting to have my arms knotted behind me while he took flying kicks at my crotch I departed to less exotic pastures.

In a barn-like Bavarian beer-hall I ordered a foaming stein of lager from a girl in a well-filled white blouse and red skirt and sat back to observe the British sailors extending the hand of friendship to the Germans.

At the table next to me a Cockney sailor with battle-scarred features was recalling his childhood during the last war.

"You know something," he said to an interested group of young Germans, "we had to buy saving stamps."

"Saving stamps?" politely.

"Yerst, saving stamps. And when we'd saved enough we were told we could buy a bomb. One day they brought a bleeding great bomb and stuck it in the town hall."

"Iss very interesting," said one of the Germans, a chill note entering his voice.

"Yerst. And do you know what I did?"

"*Nein.*"

"I got a bit of chalk and wrote HAMBURG on the bleeder."

The fight raged far into the night. It spread from the beer-hall to the farthest reaches of the red-light area. It plunged into dimly-lit clubs and sent strippers twittering into the wings; it ricocheted into brothels rudely parting hookers from their clients.

On the way back to the Four Seasons I reflected that, if only the British had organised a few good-will visits like this in 1939, the war might have been over before it started.

*   *   *

But the German trip was only a temporary respite. You could hardly construct a future based on the good offices of Andy Capp.

It was therefore in a moody frame of mind that I took the family on holiday to Dunster, a cosy town in Somerset with a broad main street lined with tea and antique shoppes, a yarn market house, three pubs and a castle. We stayed in a pink-washed pub, the Foresters' Arms, cradled by wooded slopes as still and quiet as a cathedral.

From Dunster we drove into Minehead and strolled in the evening-scented park while a band played Gilbert and Sullivan. Not for us Majorca, now £57 all-in; we were the old faithfuls brought up on two weeks of August rain, seaweed in the bedroom, loops of fairy-lights steaming in the drizzle, peppermint rock and quiet contemplation of the grey, crinkled sea from sea-front shelters where women in raincoats knitted ruminatively. What's more we couldn't afford £57 all-in.

It was in Somerset that I embarked on my hobby of collecting the worst postcards ever printed. I started with three bought in Dunster— a hoary old stag superimposed on a black and white view of Exmoor, the card stained and curling after sharing years in a showcase with the carcasses of flies; a cart-horse being led through a sepia Dunster by a sepia rustic on his way, perhaps, to visit Lady Chatterley; and a glossy gem from the thirties showing a woman with a cloche hat and pointed shoes soliciting at a corner of Ye Olde Yarn Market.

The moodiness brought on by Fleet Street's disinclination to buy my services at any price was partially dispelled by some rousing quarrels about stag-hunting in the Somerset pubs, and the flowing sense of freedom on the moors. The wind ruffling long silken grass; gorse and heather like mottled stones on the folded hills; shadows of clouds streaming through the valleys.

We drove to the Doone Valley where they charged you 6d. to walk in the footsteps of Carver Doone and 1s. to park your car; we spent a day at Butlins where, for 10s. admission, you could avail yourself of every fairground ride; we took ourselves to Weston-super-Mare, a graceless place with rows of guest-houses and a pier with a cavernous amusement arcade at the end of it. Weston had been too garish in its youth to be able to assume the dignity of old age.

Then the holiday — on which I have digressed because it was the first one I had been able to afford away from Torquay — was over and I was back in London in a rut.

One solution was to get into radio or television or both. I had never envisaged myself holding a microphone but, if newspaper editors lacked the initiative to make their overtures while I was still available, then they should be made to rue the day.

204

I had always admired TV reporters because, unlike newspaper correspondents, they had to be seen reporting while the earth quaked or the grenades exploded. I held equal respect for the sound engineers and cameramen who had to hump about equipment as heavy as a cement-overcoat in the same fraught conditions as the reporter but without the attendant glamour. It was in conditions such as these that I formed my own personalised definition of bravery.

I was in Cyprus with a posse of Pressmen who were crossing a long, low-slung bridge spanning a marsh to investigate an off-beat story in a village where, every time peace was negotiated between Greek and Turkish Cypriots, a fool with a shot-gun loosed off a charge of rusty nails and re-established hostilities.

Half way across the bridge the humour left the situation. Greeks opened up in earnest: Turks did likewise and we were caught in the cross-fire. There were no withering blasts of machine-gun fire but it only takes one bullet to give you a fatal dose of lead-poisoning.

On we plodded on either side of the road, winking at each other, teeth bared in skeletal grins, for all the world like Hollywood soldiers on their way to relieve besieged comrades.

Ahead of me marched a TV crew; behind me staffmen from Fleet Street.

Then, thank God, someone ahead shouted: "Fuck this for a game of cards," and leaped off the bridge into the marsh. We all followed suit some of us hitting the bog before the comrade who had cracked first.

And it was then that I decided that, in certain circumstances, courage was purely a matter of not wanting to make an idiot of yourself in front of your colleagues.

News reporting on radio and television was constantly under attack. Biased, slanted, angled, groaned the self-appointed critics as they stood warming their backsides in front of the fire and watching the box.

Few could have had the slightest idea of what was entailed in

205

getting film and sound from some distant, shell-torn city to the television in the lounge. Biased? If the leader of one warring faction was willing to give an interview then so be it; if the leader of his enemies declined then television or radio could hardly be expected to abandon the programme.

My favourite TV reporter was John Tidmarsh of the BBC. He was the complete pro and utterly unflappable in the most unpleasant circumstances. Not only that but, on his way to the Himalayan foothills to join me reporting the Chinese invasion of India, he brought with him a cricket bat.

I made my application for a job advertised on the BBC long before the exodus from Fleet Street to television. And I made it more out of desperation than real desire to change media because I preferred the written to the spoken word.

I filled in various forms and finally joined a short-list of candidates. While an unseen panel of judges listened, I read a short report with a false intonation that owed much to Alistair Cooke.

Then I emerged in front of the judges. An ominous looking bunch seated along a scimitar-shaped table poring over my credentials.

Finally one of them looked up, stared at me through steel-rimmed spectacles and said: "Have you ever done any radio work before?"

Was he surprised at my professionalism? "No, sir."

He nodded meaningfully, an I-thought-as-much sort of nod.

I answered several more searching questions about literature, economics and politics and spoke volubly on every subject.

The one question that really floored me was: "Mr. Lambert, have you any idea how many editions of Radio Newsreel there are?"

Obviously it wasn't one. Two was doubtful. Three my unlucky number. . . . "Eight," I said.

The questioner appraised me for a moment, either impressed by my acumen or stunned by my asininity, but said nothing more and to this day I have no idea how many editions of Radio Newsreel are broadcast.

The worst ordeal was interviewing a seasoned BBC staffman in front of the TV cameras. I have since learned that I perform passably when answering questions: it was asking them that terrified me.

The veteran staffman looked indolently assured as I launched into a rambling question about strategic arms. Sweat coursed down my face; the question seemed to last at least a minute.

At the end of it he said: "Yes."

I suppose he was under orders to make it as tough as possible for us would-be interviewers. I should like to have taken him by the neck and shaken him vigorously shouting: "Yes what?" But I was being tested for greater things; it would hardly do to grasp a visiting Head of State by the neck.

"Yes, ah, I see. Mmm." I embarked on another question which seemed to have no logical end to it. I let the words spill out waiting for some sort of interrogative conclusion. Finally I stopped, unsure whether or not I had asked a question.

This seemed to equally confuse my subject. If he said: "Could you repeat the question?" I would beat him about the head with the microphone. But he didn't. Instead he plunged into an answer of horrendous length which seemed to have little relevance to my question.

"I'm afraid time's running out. . . ." I began. But it had no affect on the torrent of words. "I'm afraid I shall have to cut you short. . . ."

"What?"

"Cut you short."

"Oh if you must," he said, and stopped.

"Thank you very much. This is Derek Lambert from the BBC studios in London returning you to the BBC studios in London."

I left the studios without even bothering to consult anyone. I had blown it.

But ever since, I have always had the utmost compassion for

the television interviewer. And for the news-reader who announces with aplomb that we are now going over to another location — while the camera remains steadfastly trained on his twitching features. At times like these I have to grovel behind the sofa until his ordeal is over.

*   *   *

Meanwhile back at the *Mirror* I felt like a serpent among my colleagues — although I had spotted one of them hiding behind a potted palm while I was awaiting my interview at the BBC. All I could do was buckle down.

But I wasn't too proud to chase fire-engines and ambulances on my way home. That way I picked up one or two late-night stories and attracted the attentions of the police who assumed that I had been listening to their messages on the VHF band of the radio.

It was illegal to act on these broadcasts and the police occasionally put out fictitious messages. When an enterprising free-lance arrived at the scene of a non-existent crime they pinched him.

On those late night occasions I also learned how to telephone the office if you didn't have enough pennies. The trick was to use halfpennies, insert them into the coin box at an angle and give them a hefty smack with your hand. Other reporters, even more criminally inclined, knew how to back-dial or tap out a number on the rest beneath the receiver.

The alternative if you were in a deserted, rain-swept street was to transfer the charges which seemed ridiculous when only pennies were involved. Not only that but it could take a lifetime to raise the operator and then you would listen, frantic to dictate your copy, while this sort of conversation ensued.

"*Daily Mirror.*"

"Are you Holborn 4321?"

"We are."

"Will you accept a transfer-charge call from a Mr. Lambert?"

208

"Where's he speaking from?" expecting a call from Outer Mongolia or Chad.

"Brixton."

"Brixton?" incredulously.

"Yes," firmly, "Brixton."

"God almighty, the last of the big spenders. Put him on."

A journalist is often asked what he believes to be the essential qualifications of his calling. The last few paragraphs obliquely illustrate one of the requirements.

The journalist — or at least the general news reporter on a daily paper — must be prepared to allow his profession to intrude into almost every aspect of his life. On the journey home when the fire-engine clangs past; on holiday when a story breaks in his cloistered retreat; in bed in the depths of exhausted sleep when the telephone rings.

More important, he must welcome these intrusions: he must want to participate in the infinite variations of human behaviour and to chronicle them.

If he is emotionally involved he must be dispassionate in his reporting but never cynical. Journalistic cynicism is a Hollywood misinterpretation of accrued wisdom: the true cynic wouldn't last five editions on a newspaper because his curiosity would be atrophied.

Curiosity, then, is indispensable. The reporter must have the crossword-puzzle addict's determination to fill in all the blank squares and must never allow himself to be affected by diversionary tactics.

Threats ("I happen to know your editor"), physical violence, preposterous lies, evasive action, appeals to the reporter's compassion, statements penned with distilled fog. . . . All these weapons and more will be mobilised to silence the journalist seeking truth.

He must always remember that, when such backs-to-the wall manoeuvres are employed, there is almost certainly something worth viewing over the top of that wall.

Sometimes the Press attracts justifiable criticism. These lapses should be considered in their right perspective. A free

Press with all its faults is far more preferable than a Press shackled to a tyranny, which is what any country without freedom of speech becomes.

In my experience the battle hymns of those crusading for curtailment of Press liberty have always contained a few discords of self-interest.

*　　*　　*

The majority of stories I covered on the *Mirror* could not be recognised immediately as part of the structure of democracy. But they were just that because they were a daily reminder to politicians, financiers, policemen, anyone in a position of authority, that a watchdog was on the loose safe-guarding the interests of those unaware of their rights.

We home-based news reporters snapped at the heels of injustice: the leader-writers, columnists and specialists delivered the body blows.

But now I smelled the snow over the steppes, saw the lights of Manhattan from the top of the Empire State Building, heard the rhythms of the African night. . . .

During one such mood of lyrical frustation I telephoned the news editor of the *Daily Express*, a shrewd and ebullient North Countryman named Keith Howard, and having exhausted my meagre resources of pride, told him that I wanted a job.

There was a pause. Then he said: "I thought you'd never ask. I'd heard you wanted to join us. Six-thirty at the Punch."

At 6.25 p.m. I sidled into the Punch, an old-fashioned pub with a good line in pork pies, where Keith Howard conducted his hire-or-fire operations. I crouched over a half-pint hoping that no *Mirror* men had observed my furtive entry and wondering whether Keith Howard would be more impressed by a sober, half-pint scribe or a large-Scotch-man-of-the-world.

"What'll you have?" he said, breezing in and ordering himself a gin-and-tonic.

"A pint of bitter, please," I said, compromising.

Keith, ginger-haired and burly, had himself been a reporter in the North and for much of the time we discussed mutual acquaintances, particularly the *bon viveurs* of the Liverpool Press Club.

Half way through the conversation it occurred to me that he was giving me an object lesson in interviewing. Interspersed between the niceties, smoothly inserted so that they seemed part of the discussion, were such questions as: "What do you think makes an *Expressman*?"

I navigated the expert interrogation successfully because he took my home telephone number and told me he would be in touch. He was — next day.

At 3.30 p.m. I presented myself at the shining black head-quarters of the *Express* in Fleet Street — entering with a swag-ger because there was no way you could disguise the reason for such a visit -- and was immediately escorted by lift to the office of the editor, Bob Edwards.

Bob Edwards was a lithe, dapper journalist with springy hair like mine; he restlessly paced his office and, such was the impression of suppressed energy, that I shouldn't have been surprised to see him emitting sparks.

The interview was brief. Five minutes after entering the *Express* portals I had been taken on the staff.

That evening I wrote an inarticulate letter trying to explain to Ken Hord why I had decided to leave and expressing my gratitude for all the help, compassion and instruction he had extended in my direction.

He wrote a two-paragraph reply which reached me the same evening via his secretary Dot Watson. The reply thanked me for my services and wished me well in the future. They never tried to persuade you to stay on the *Mirror*; nor would they ever have you back.

As he walked past my desk, holding hat and umbrella, he paused, stuck out one hand and said: "Good luck, chum," and was gone to join the homeward crowds, one of the least likely but one of the most accomplished news editors in the game. Dot Watson embraced me and wept a little.

Few journalists worked out their notice. The decision was made, the contract immediately terminated. That night in Barney Finnegans I celebrated and mourned; good years gone, challenge ahead.

Throughout the evening I listened drunkenly to speculation about the increase in salary I was to receive. The highest bid was another thirty pounds a week. Two quid would have been more like it.

The following week I began work on the *Daily Express*. I was exactly half way through my Fleet Street career which was to culminate in Moscow.

Other best-sellers
by Derek Lambert . . .

The Saint Peter's Plot

As the Russians and the Western Allies race towards Berlin, the Nazi hierarchy plots to escape the inevitable retribution facing them at the end of World War II.

With chilling authenticity, Derek Lambert reveals for the first time the seething hot-bed of spies and intrigue that was centered inside the sanctimonious walls of The Vatican City – in the midst of German-occupied Rome – during the closing stages of the War, and the controversial double role played by The Vatican itself in harbouring both Jewish refugees and high-ranking Nazi war criminals.

Two men hold the key.

Father Liam Doyle, an American-Irish priest, is tormented by conflicting loyalties; his spiritual devotion to God and his love for the beautiful, passionate Jewess, Maria Reubeni, who persuades him to help the Jews find refuge within The Vatican.

Kurt Wolff is the handsome, blond SS Captain and a member of Hitler's personal elitist bodyguard, whose credentials are impeccable; blindly devoted to the Fuhrer and to the cause of the Third Reich, and bestowed with many honours for his almost inhuman bravery and loyalty. Yet he has still to know the greatest honour of all. He has been chosen to implement Grey Fox – *The Saint Peter's Plot* – the most daring and secret mission of the War. As Germany stands on the edge of an abyss, the fate of this once great nation is in his hands . . .

Price £4.95   ISBN 85140 289 5

The Memory Man

As he swung his Ferrari into the turn he realised he was in trouble; the angle was too sharp and his brakes had just given out. From the sharp pang of fear, the smell of burning rubber and dark oblivion he finds himself looking down on a group of men in operating gowns huddled over a body shrouded on a table. That body was himself. He then feels a release, a feeling of knowing what lay beyond and readily succumbs to the happiness that he knows awaits him.

Martin Fox, champion Formula One racing driver, is living in New York recuperating from a near fatal accident. Selena Porter also waits for his strength to return and, hopefully with it, his love. She doesn't realise that something else has taken hold of him, a new obsession. Had he experienced life after death?

Karl Dorfman, an anaesthetist, has come close to life after death in the operating room and feels that with a little help the age old riddle of what lies beyond can be solved. But with two fatalities on his record he has to experiment in private. He finds the perfect subject in Raymond Hohl, the one time Memory Man, now full time loser.

Detective Sergeant William Schaeffer, while trying to unravel the mystery of a series of murders that is terrorising the back streets and cheap bars of New York, finds himself getting more and more involved with these men and their obscure pursuit.

Derek Lambert has once again produced a hard-hitting thriller that skilfully embodies the question that has tormented man for centuries: Is there life after death?

Price £5.25   ISBN 85140 327 1

Touch The Lion's Paw

Ten times a year an executive jet leaves London Airport bound for Antwerp. Under heavy guard in those ten flights are millions of pounds of rough diamonds being shipped from London's diamond centre, Hatton Garden, for cutting and consignment in Antwerp, the centre of the world's diamond industry. Each consignment is valued between £13 and £15 million.

Around these true facts Derek Lambert has created his most intriguing novel. Johnny Rhodes, a retired and restless jewel thief, is pondering marriage, vaguely displeased with his spreading waistline. He hears about the shipments from Antwerp and decides to postpone retirement in order to carry out one last robbery.

Rhodes needs assistance, and he eventually recruits a man named Pierre Tallon from Marseilles, now retired but who had achieved notoriety by organising some of the great wine frauds of this century. The trio is completed with the addition of a former (but very classy) cat burglar from Harlem named Moses Ferguson.

There is just one flaw in Rhode's plan. Tallon has been having a difficult time adjusting to his contact lenses, and Ferguson can't shake a nagging knee injury. As for Rhodes, he still isn't in top shape. But despite these decidedly middle-age afflictions, the trio proceeds with its plans, and the reader is drawn into the fascinating and shadowy world of the diamond trade. Written with expert knowledge, *Touch The Lion's Paw* is a highly entertaining novel.

Now a major film starring Burt Reynolds and David Niven and retitled *Rough Cut*.

Price £4.95   ISBN 85140 240 2

Don't Quote Me . . . But

Don't Quote Me . . . But covers the hilarious apprenticeship of a former foreign correspondent – now a best-selling author – years before he date-lined his newspaper stories from the trouble-spots of the world.

Derek Lambert's first scoop, when he was a cub-reporter on a provincial weekly, got him fired on his twenty-first birthday – the outbreak of smallpox which he had exclusively reported turned out to be chicken-pox! He sent agonised football pool treble-chancers into hysterics by failing to telephone a drawn result in time for the BBC classified broadcast; he conspired with a village police constable, accused by Headquarters of failing to arrest anyone for a decade, to catch two burglars; he solved the baffling mysteries of the amateur operatic baritone's voice, which always changed pitch half way through the *Indian Love Call*, and the mutilation of a Colonel's prize-winning marrow at the Annual Horticultural Show. These are just a few examples of the many entertaining stories contained in this book. *Don't Quote Me . . . But* does for cub reporters what James Herriott has done for vets.

But Derek Lambert's early experiences are not merely anecdotal; his recollections provide a vivid insight into the production of local newspapers that will delight laymen and enthrall all those young men and women who want to become Pressmen. *Don't Quote Me . . . But* ends as Lambert, whose sights have always been set on Fleet Street, joins a national newspaper.

Price £4.50   ISBN 85140 284 4